W9-CUT-160

Rumi's Little Book of Love

Other titles by the same authors

Whispers of the Beloved
Hidden Music

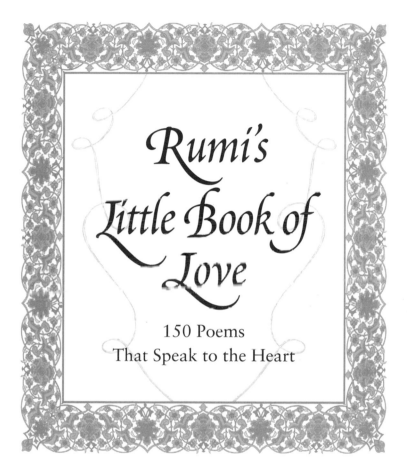

Rumi's Little Book of Love

150 Poems
That Speak to the Heart

Maryam Mafi and Azima Melita Kolin

Hampton Roads
Publishing Company, Inc.

Cover art and jacket design by Richard Wehrman

Hampton Roads Publishing Company, Inc.
PO Box 8107
Charlottesville, VA 22906

434-296-2772
fax: 434-296-5096
e-mail: hrpc@hrpub.com
www.hrpub.com

If you are unable to order this book from your local
bookseller, you may order directly from the publisher.
Call 434-296-2772.

ISBN 978-0-9818771-2-9
1 3 5 7 9 10 8 6 4 2
Printed and bound by Leo, China

Contents

Introduction

Rumi – Mowlana Jalaludin Mohamad – one of the most revered mystical poets of all times, was born on 30 September 1207 in Balkh. As the Mogul invasion of the Persian Empire drew near, Rumi and his family moved to Konya in Turkey, where he lived until his death on 17 December 1273. A descendant of a long line of Islamic scholars, Rumi was educated in the Sufi tradition by his father and his followers. Upon his father's death, Rumi, still in his early twenties, took over the position as head of the theological school in Konya, which had been specifically created for his father by the local ruler. He excelled in all theological fields and acquired many devoted followers.

In 1244 Rumi met Shams of Tabriz, a wandering dervish and a highly advanced spiritual master, who set fire to Rumi's heart and revealed to him the direct path to the Beloved. The intensity of their encounter led to Rumi's forsaking his school and students, which resulted in great resentment on their part.

Shams and Rumi did not have much time together – perhaps only two-and-a-half years – before Shams disappeared from Rumi's life. Some say Shams was murdered by Rumi's jealous

followers; some believe that he left because he knew he could teach Rumi nothing more. After Shams' disappearance Rumi, in search of his ultimate Beloved, turned to poetry to express the pain of his loss; he became a lover, a poet par excellence, a dervish, a mystic. No one has ever understood who was the student and who was the master.

Rumi's colossal volume, *Divan of Shams of Tabriz*, contains 3500 odes and almost 2000 quatrains. His monumental *Masnavi* is a six-volume treasury of teaching poems, containing over 25,000 verses in which he uses the media of story, tale and anecdote to explore the multifaceted layers of spiritual wisdom. His *Fi ma Fihi*, or *Discourses*, gathered into a book by his followers after his death, is a collection of lectures, comments, sermons and conversations on a variety of subjects directly affecting the everyday life of man and his relationship with the divine.

Gardens appear in many of Rumi's poems; they are symbols depicting the inner spaces of the soul, heart and spirit. Sometimes the poems take us through gardens filled with the nightingale's song and the scent of roses in springtime; sometimes we are taken through gardens filled with the sorrow of winter. At times challenging, at other times comforting, they are pathways on the inner journey of the soul that open doors to unimaginable wonders, drawing back branches to reveal hidden secrets.

Rumi's Beloved has many gardens; some are visible, some are shrouded in mystery. As we wend our way in and out of these gardens, Rumi takes us through the shattering pain of separation and longing on a journey of bewilderment. His poems weave an intricate web between our image of ourselves and our innermost self.

Rumi: Gardens of the Beloved is a collection of 150 quatrains, selected from the *Divan*, that depict the delicate stages of our spiritual journey. In ever-changing shades of darkness and light along the way, we are carried on the wings of his words to the safe place of no-place. Rumi has been a source of inspiration for centuries. His poetry is all-inclusive, transcending all forms to reach the realm of essence. Rumi opens our inner eye and pierces our heart with the light of Truth. Only then do we see that we are merely '... a brush in the hand of the Master Painter'.

The Soul Is Our Guide

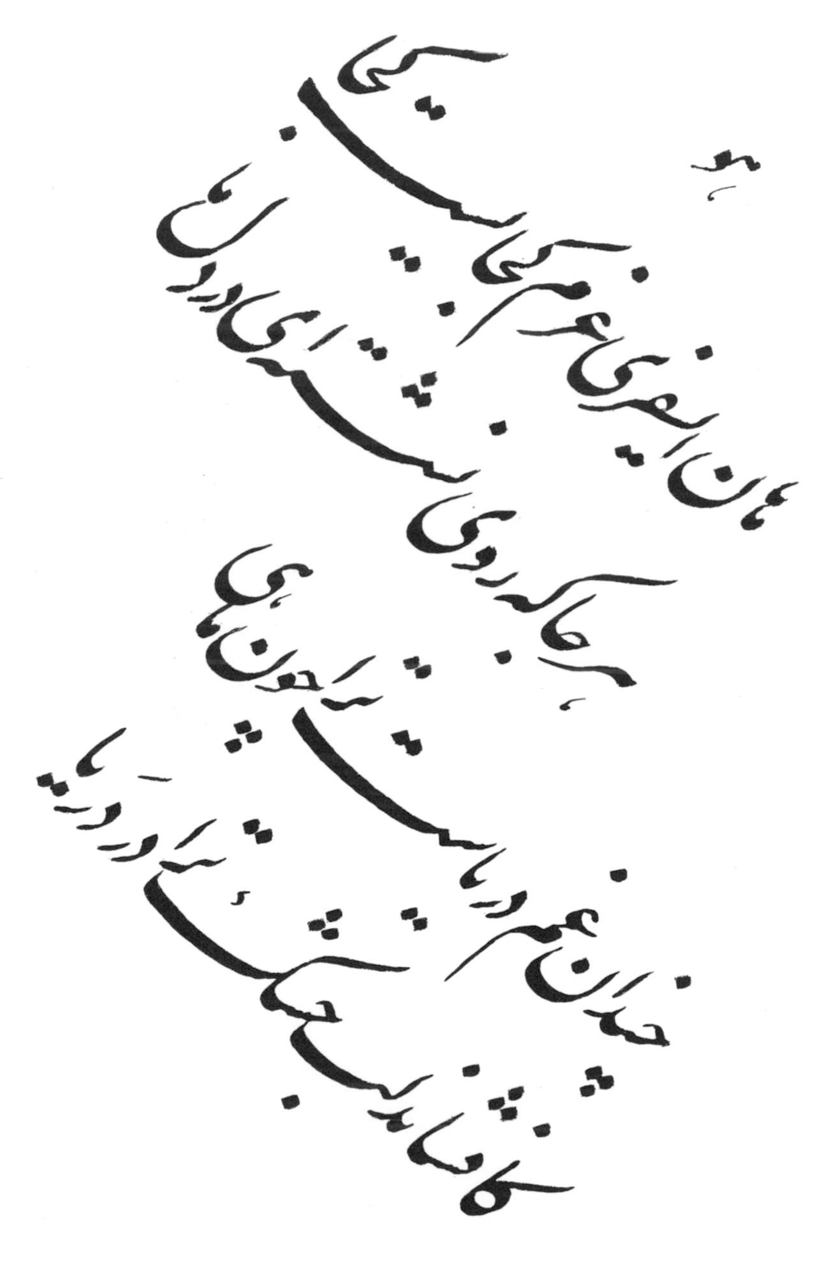

Where are you going my dear traveller,
longing for the sea like a fish?
You are in my heart wherever you go,
only that sea can quench your thirst.

Do not be idle, you will either eat
or sleep too much.
When you hear the music
of the whirling lovers, leap
and join their circle.

Indulging in our pride we keep chasing
after every fleeting image.
How strange that, being nothing,
we cultivate such grand illusions!

When you stop admiring yourself
and let the eyes of the heart
open your vision to vast other worlds
then all you do, will become admirable.

The secret of Truth is not unravelled
by questioning or giving away
your wealth and position.
You cannot exalt the heart with mere words,
pain is the price that the heart has to pay.

One needs to be strong
to bear the burning pain of longing;
rushing towards Union is not the answer.
It is in the state of separation that
all one's strength is needed.

No one could solve my dilemma
nor could they tell me where I come from.
Now, lost at the crossroads
my heart bleeds, wondering
which way is home.

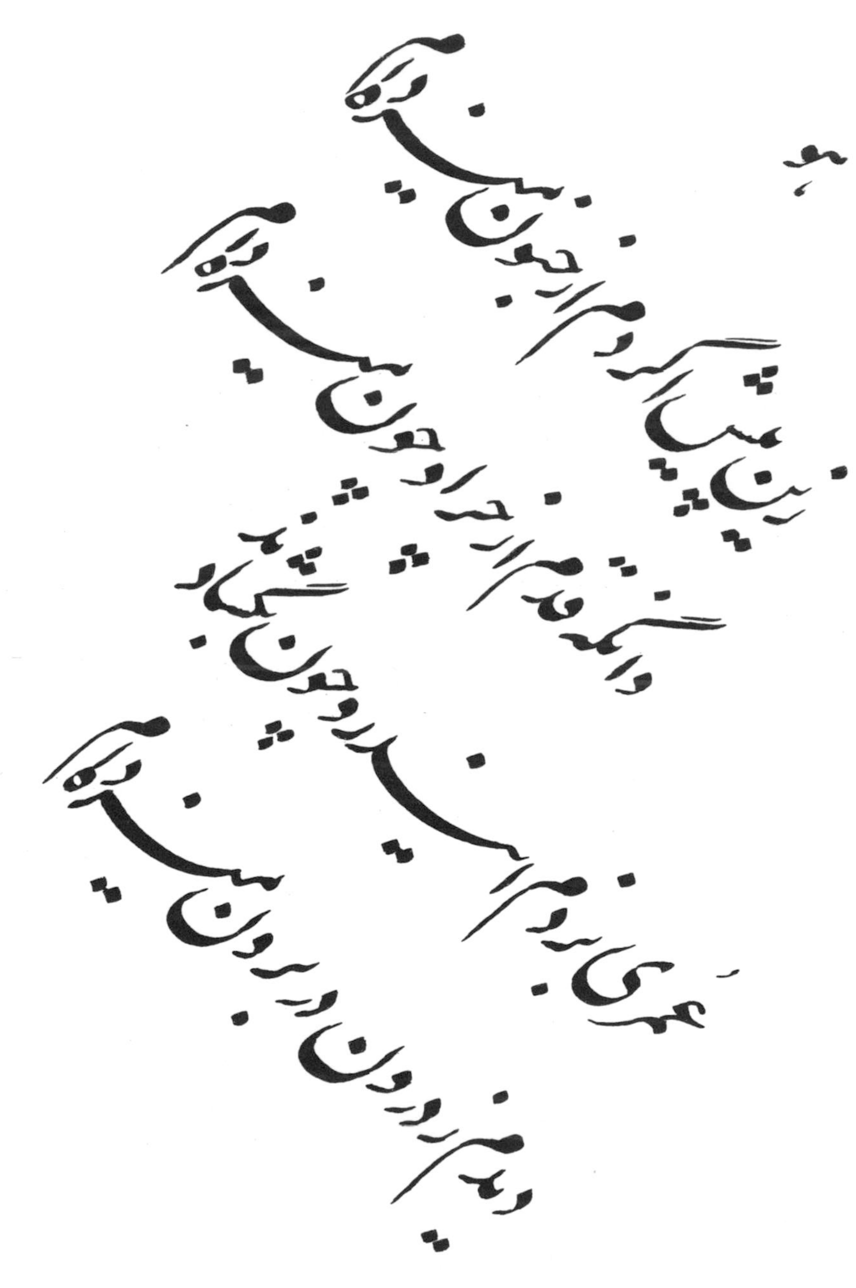

Troubled by questions all my life,
like a madman I have been
knocking at the door.
It opened!
I had been knocking from inside.

You brought release to the tormented
and offered the cup of joy to the sorrowful,
but they have long forgotten.
Tell me, if you are not to offer them the cup again,
what were you trying to teach them?

You come late to those lost in love
but when you do, you come with all your might;
gentle as a deer or regal as a lion,
but never without your piercing sword.

Sometimes you turn a deaf ear to my pleas,
and do not allow me even to kiss your feet.
It matters not if you drown or burn me,
for You are my ultimate Master.

Ever since you fled from my embrace
no one has seen me without tears.
You are always in my heart and soul;
I hope you, too, will not forget me.

Oh how lonely it is out on God's sea
with no shore in sight!
We, like ships and clouds in the night,
navigate only by the grace of His light.

I filled the garden with candles tonight,

set the table with wine and sweets

and called the musicians.

How I wish that you could be here!

I died once but no one shed a tear,
so if I live again I will know how to be.
You pursue me with your ignorant talk
which to me sounds so empty.

Time will silence the clamour of pride
that fills the head of every man.
The wolf of nothingness
will tear the flock apart
and the flood of death
will carry everything away.

Who can uplift our soul?
The One who gave us life, the King
who at times covers the eyes of his falcon
and at times lifts the hood and looses it to its prey.

It is said that God's light
comes from six directions.
"From where?" asks the crowd,
turning left and right.
If only you could look neither way
for a moment.

A cave is hidden within you
and beyond it, unimaginable wonders.
Everybody has a job and a lover but
the hidden Lover is the most wondrous.

When life ends we are given another.
Love is the water of Eternal Life;
when you enter that immense sea,
you will know that each drop of it
brims with Life.

My heart, on this path words are hollow.
At the door of Union
you have to surrender yourself.
You will never soar to the sky
where His birds fly
unless you give up your wings.

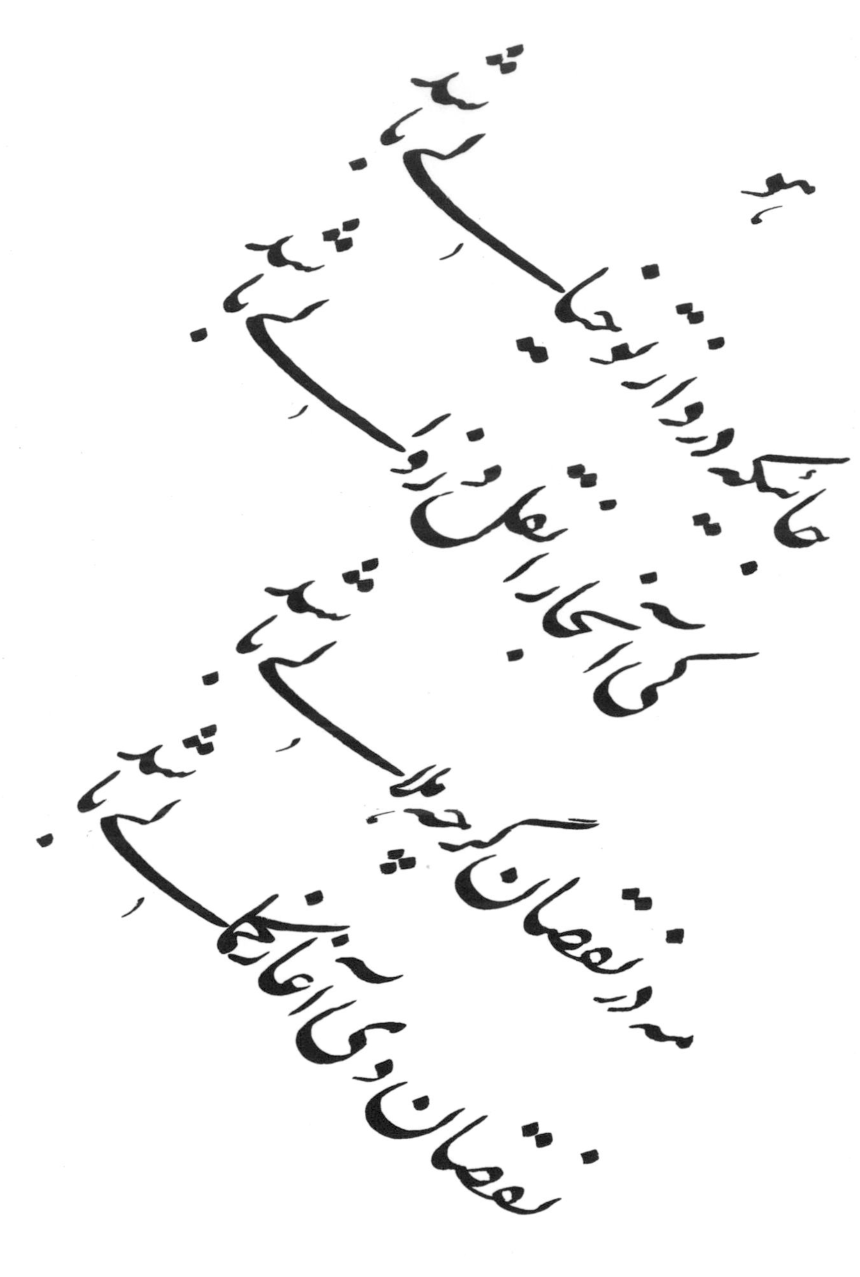

A soul that carries your image, beloved
never withers nor fades.
The slim crescent of the moon signals
only the beginning of fullness.

My dear soul, flee from the worthless,
stay close only to those with a pure heart.
Like attracts like.
A crow will lead you to the graveyard,
a parrot to a lump of sugar.

The wisdom of Truth manifests suddenly
but only in a heart that is aware.
The King does not appear unless
one is emptied of the self.

I said, "Show me what to do."
He said, *Die*.
I said, "The water has turned into oil."
He said, *Die*.
I said, "I will become a butterfly
circling around your light."
He said, *Die*.

I will never allow myself
to be the object of your mockery,
treacherous ones!
My contempt can bring such devastation
that you may never recover.

You came suddenly and stole
three things from me:
the patience from my heart,
the colour from my face
and the sleep from my eyes.
Oh, I bless the hand that
no mind can conceive!

You come from the celestial spheres
but, seduced by this clay form
you believe you belong to the earth.
Why have you forsaken that
which is your essence?

هو

درویشان را عار بود محتشمی
وندر دلشان بار بود محتشمی
اندر ره دوست فقر مطلق حشمست
کاندر ره او خوار بود محتشمی

Prosperity and rank
are a heavy burden for a dervish.
In his practice of absolute poverty
he beholds the greatness of the Beloved.

To dance is not to jump to your feet at once
and rise painlessly in the air like dust.
To rise above both worlds
is to dance in the blood of your pain
and give up your life.

It is your desires that lure you further away
from your quest for the Beloved.
If you are seeking Union,
you must enter the garden of longing.

Although the road is never ending
take a step and keep walking,
do not look fearfully into the distance.
On this path let the heart be your guide
for the body is hesitant and full of fear.

We are in love with Love
because Love is our salvation.
Our guide is the Soul
and Love, the water of life.
Woe to him who cannot find the source
for his path is barred by his own ignorance.

You stepped on the ground
and the earth, pregnant with joy,
gave birth to infinite blossoms.
The cheering spread up to heaven!
The moon glanced amazed at the stars.

The two worlds we imagine
are just a dwelling place
from which we come and go.
The many stories
we have heard about the soul
are just fairy tales.

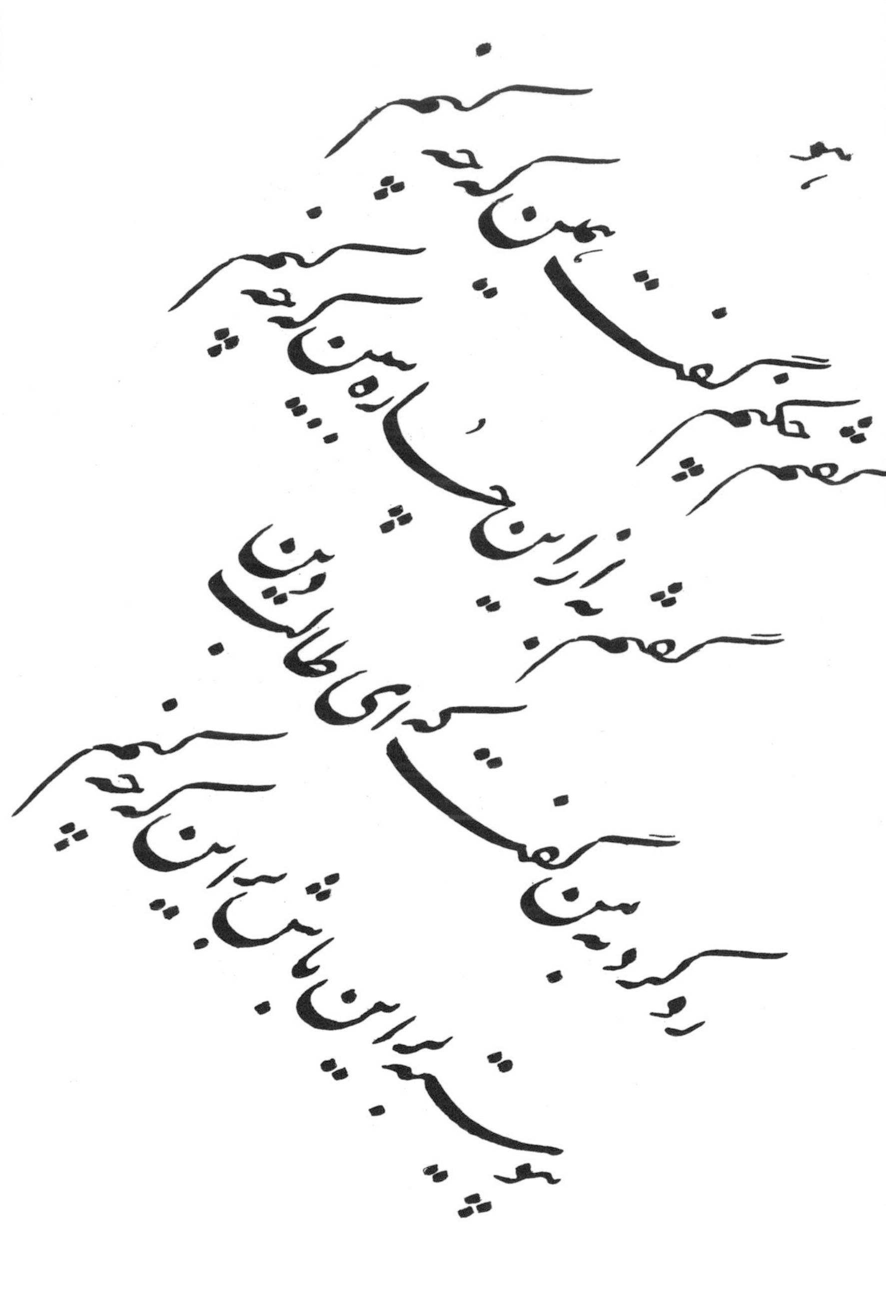

I asked, "What should I do?"

He said, *That is the question.*

I said, "Is this all you can say?"

He said, *Seeker, always keep asking,*

"What should I do?"

Do not fear, there is always wine
if you are thirsty for love.
Do not fear, there is always water
if your lips are parched.
Do not fear your ruin, inside you
there is a treasure.
Open your eyes, for this world
is only a dream.

We have stolen the moonlight
and brought it into the garden
to shake the sleep off the flowers.
Wake up, our ship has been ice-bound
long enough, the time has come
to sail the open seas.

Stay under the shadow of the lovers
for the glare of the sun will burn you up.
Stay close to them and under their protection
one day, like the sun, you will begin to shine.

In the darkness of the night
You pitched the tent of the moon
and sprinkled water
on the face of wisdom as it slept.
You promised everyone relief, yet
with the sword of longing
You struck off the head of sleep.

Sleep, my friend, but if you do
the light of Truth will slip by you unnoticed.
Asleep in the darkness of the night
you will miss the splendour of the dawn.

My heart, if you want to sit by a thorn,
what can I do?
If you do not want to pick flowers
what can I do?
If you do not see His beauty
illuminating the world,
what can I do?

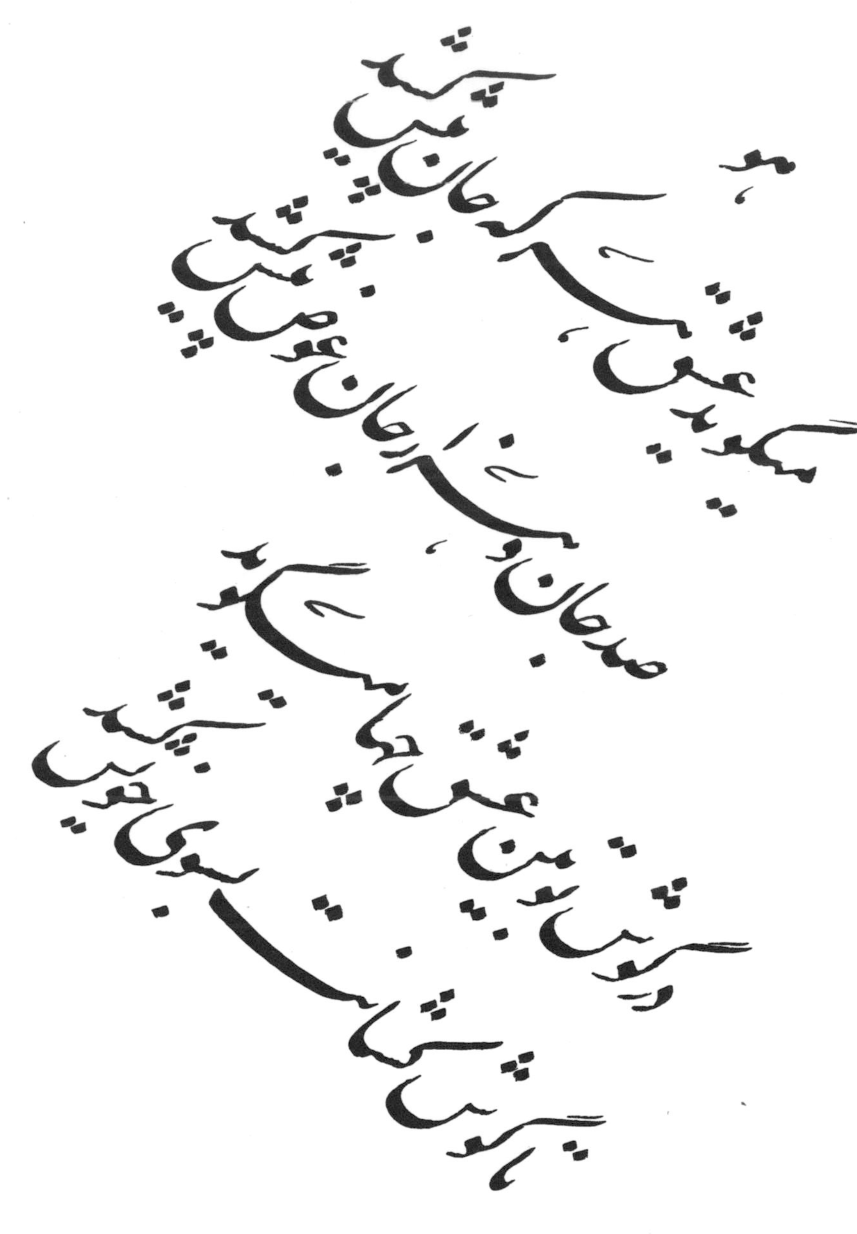

Love promises
that if you give one life
you will receive thousands in return.
Listen carefully
for it is Love's way
pulling you by the ear
closer to herself.

Your body is woven
from the light of heaven.
Are you aware
that its purity and swiftness
is the envy of the angels
and its courage
keeps even devils away.

Days and nights
I have spent in hope,
Your face has never left me.
Now that my life has passed
my hope will outlive me.

Everyone has someone:
a friend, a lover, some skill or work.
But I am alone
with the dream of my Beloved
hidden in the corner of my heart.

When the wine of love is fermenting,
each night we are drawn to the tavern
to sit amongst the lovers,
for it is only they who will recognise us.

My heart,
do not let the rust of sorrow near you,
do not waste time in superficial company.
When you become satisfied with little
you will belittle the world.

Where is the moon that never rises nor sets?
Is the spirit within or without?
Stop this nonsense and let us speak straight!
The whole world is Him but tell me,
where are your eyes?

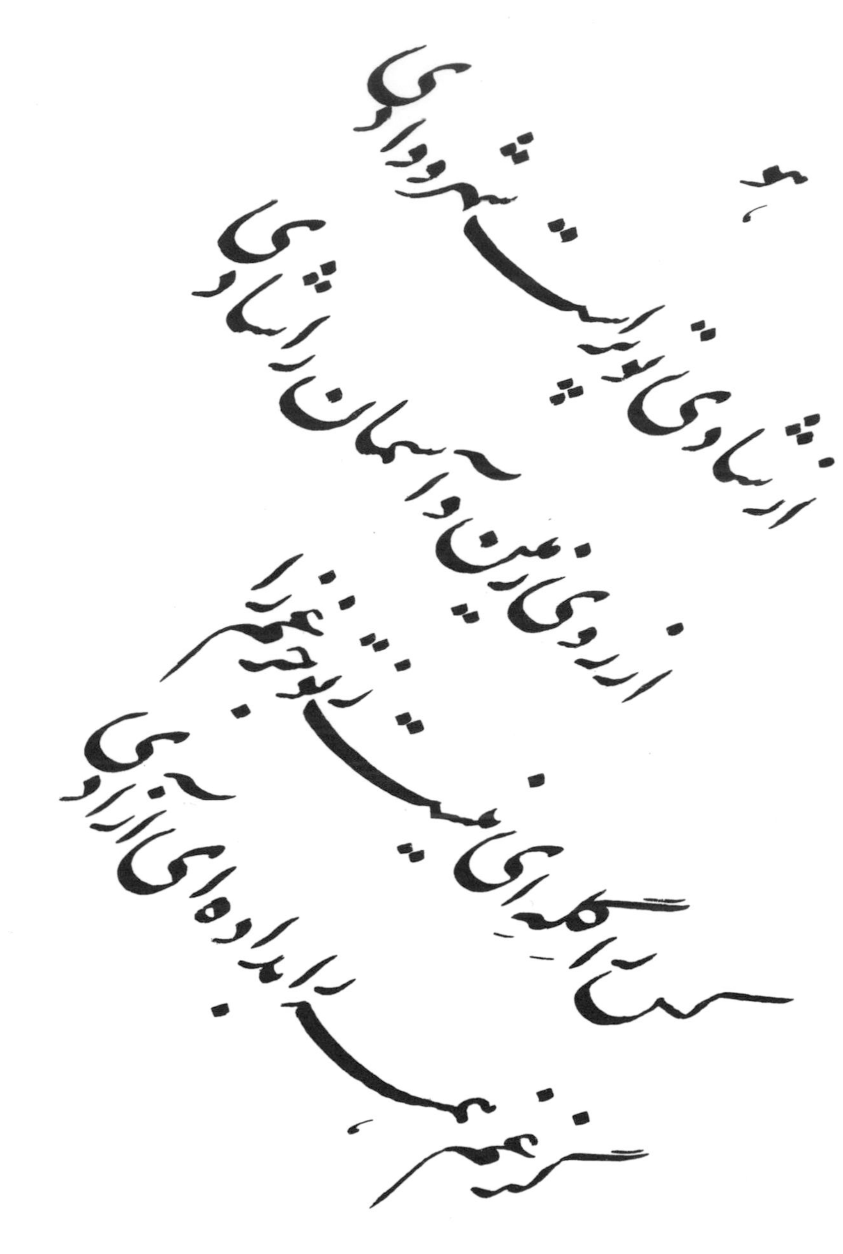

Joy has taken over the entire town,
even the sky and the earth are in bliss.
Only sorrow is complaining
because You have freed
everyone from it.

I Threw My Heart to the Winds

The dew of love
turned a lump of clay into a man
and the whole world was stirred.
A hundred lances pierced
the veins of Spirit;
one drop fell on Earth
and we named it Heart.

هو

در باغ هزار شاهد مه‌رو بود

گلها و بنفشه‌های مشکین بو بود

وان آب زره زره که اندر جو بود

این جمله بهانه بود و او خود او بود

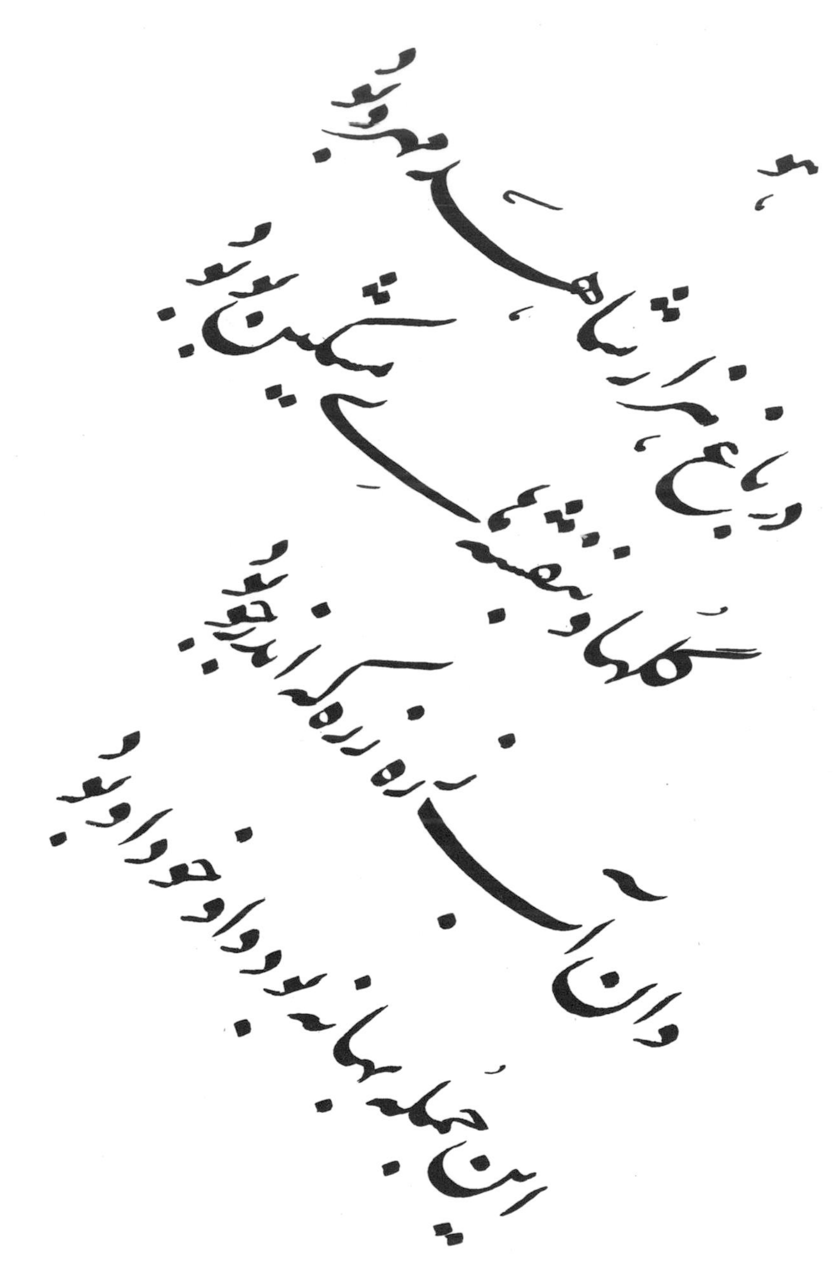

A thousand beauties fill the garden:
the scent of roses,
the murmur of water
gently flowing in the stream …
But how can one describe
the indescribable?

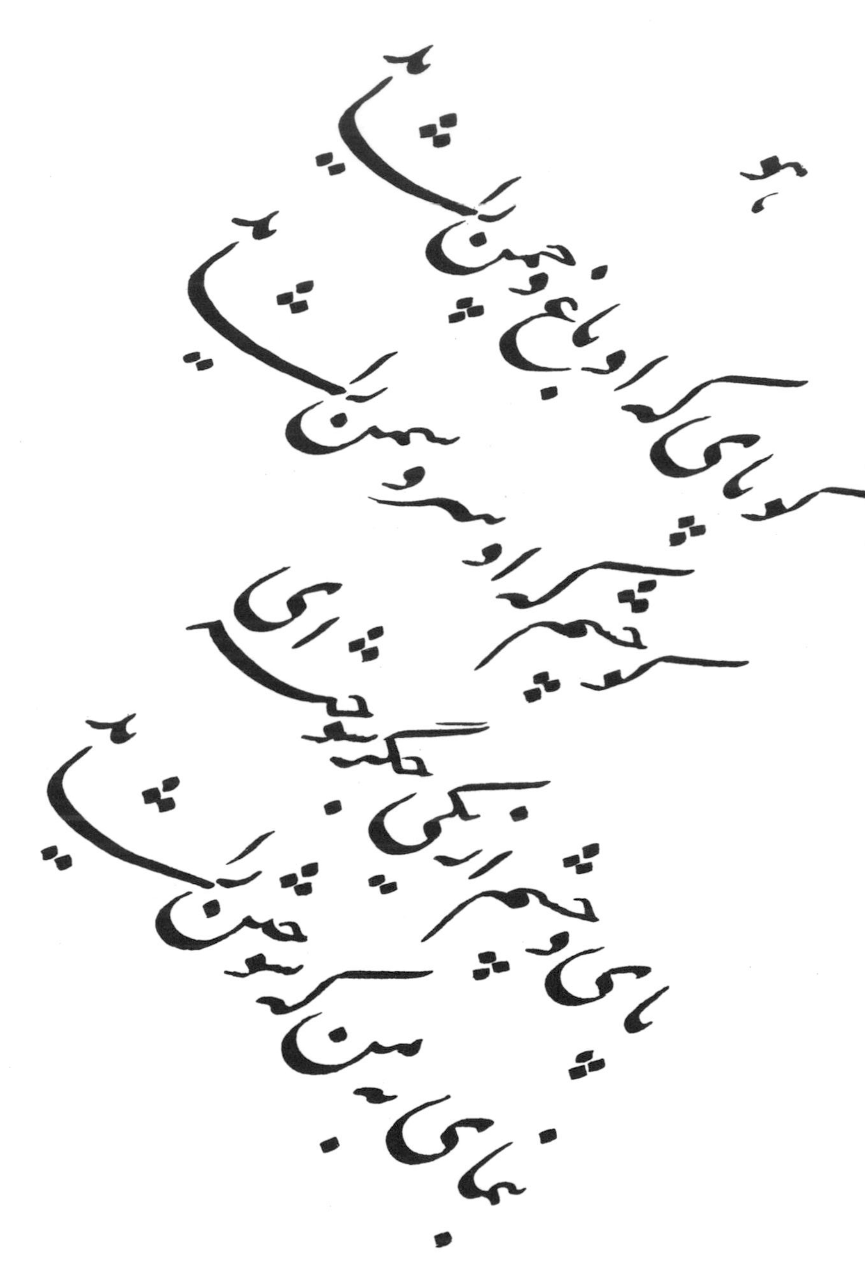

Whose feet are worthy
to enter the garden?
Whose eyes are worthy
of the cypress and the jasmine?
The feet and eyes of a heart
that has been broken.

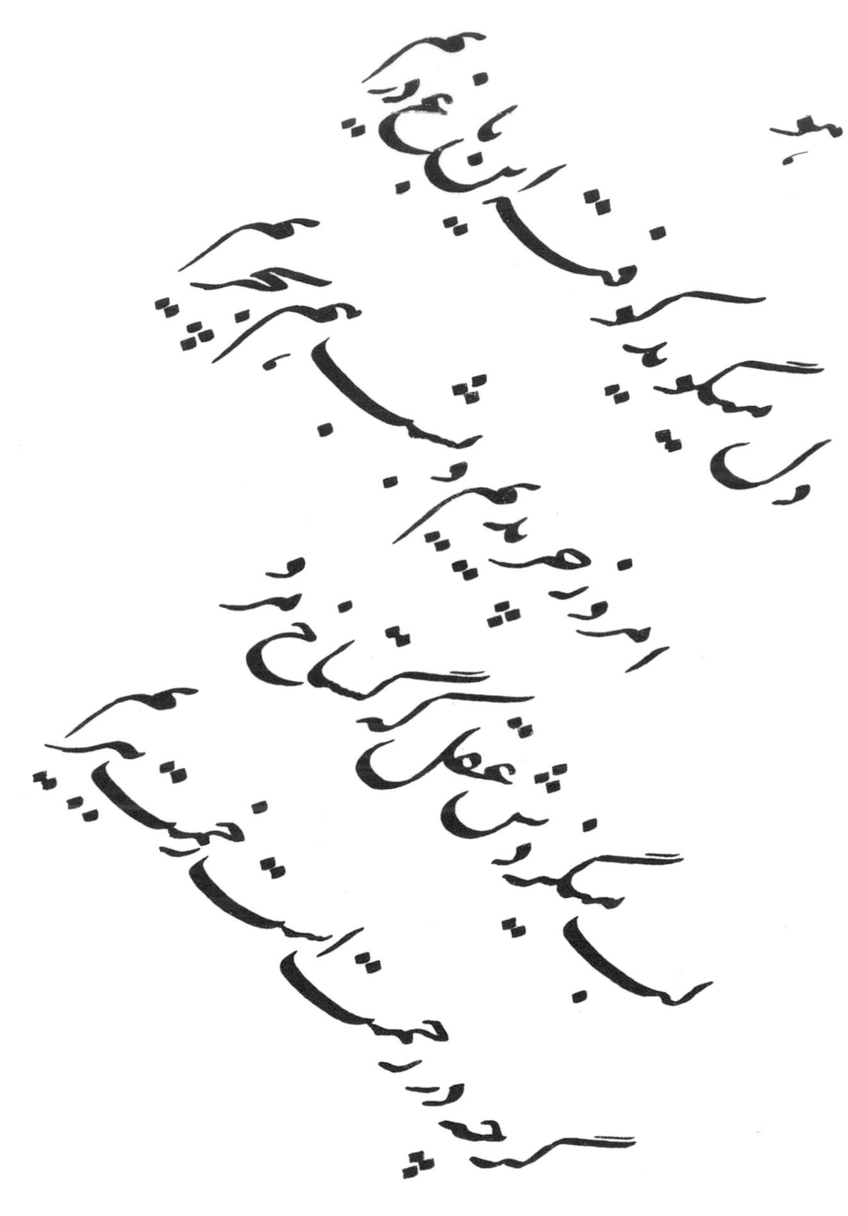

My heart rushes into the garden,
joyfully tasting all the delights.
But reason frowns, disapproving
of the heart's bad manners.

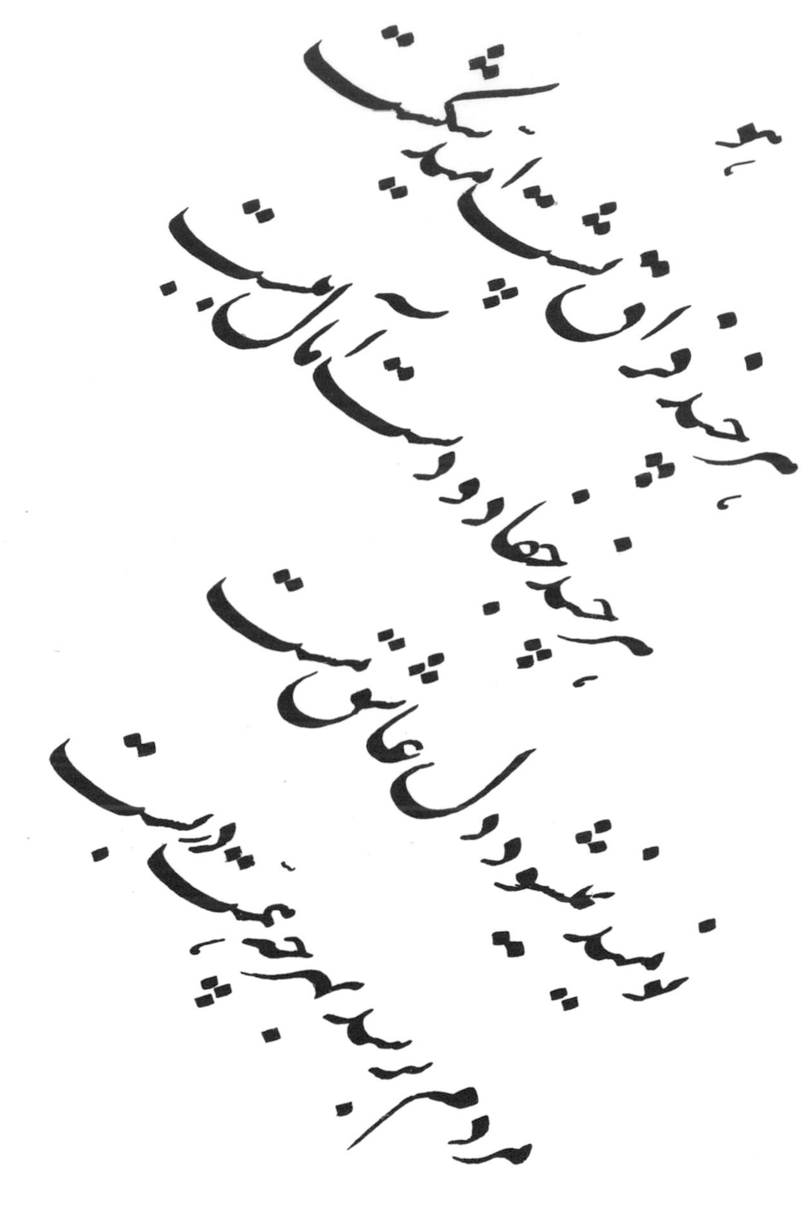

The back of hope
is bent by separation,
the hands of longing
tied by cruelty
but the lover never despairs.
For a committed heart
everything is possible.

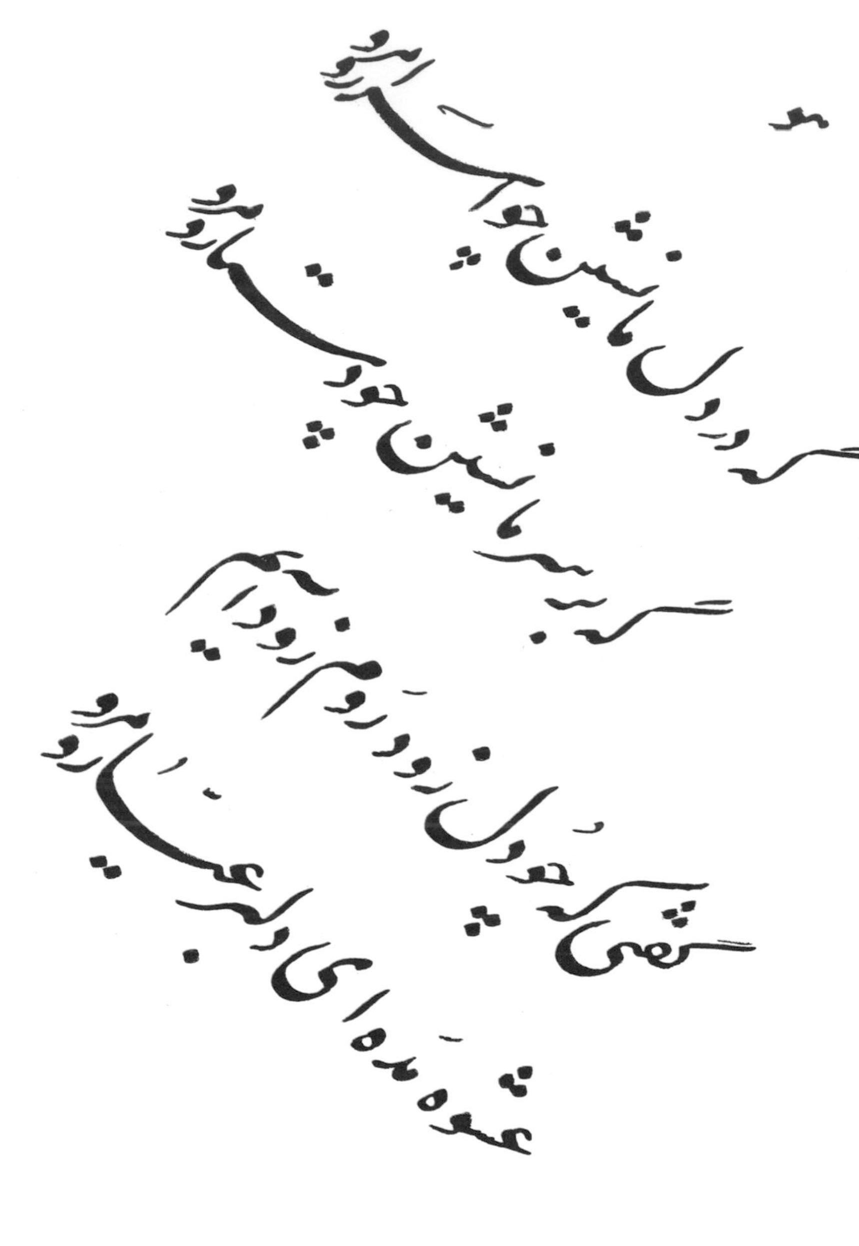

Do not leave me,
hide in my heart like a secret,
wind around my head like a turban.
"I come and go as I please,"
you say, "swift as a heartbeat."
You can tease me as much as you like
but never leave me.

Why does sorrow turn around the heart?
Do sad and cold hearts attract it?
For a loving heart is an immense sea,
with waves that make
the tallest domes whirl.

Tell the morning breeze
that you have seen my fiery heart.
Tell her that my heart's passion
has burned all the thorns on my path.

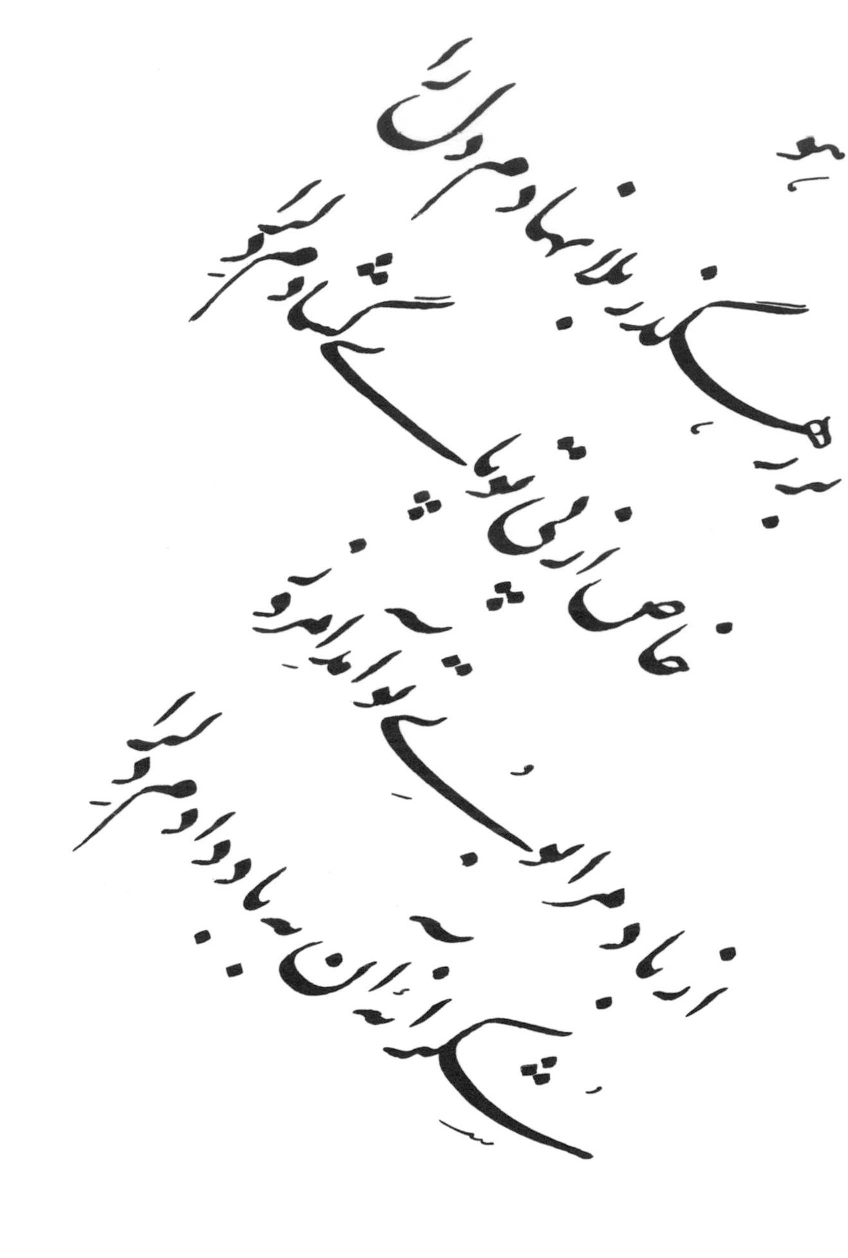

I threw my heart to the winds
and followed you.
One day the wind brought me your scent,
my heart swelled in gratitude
and scattered in the wind.

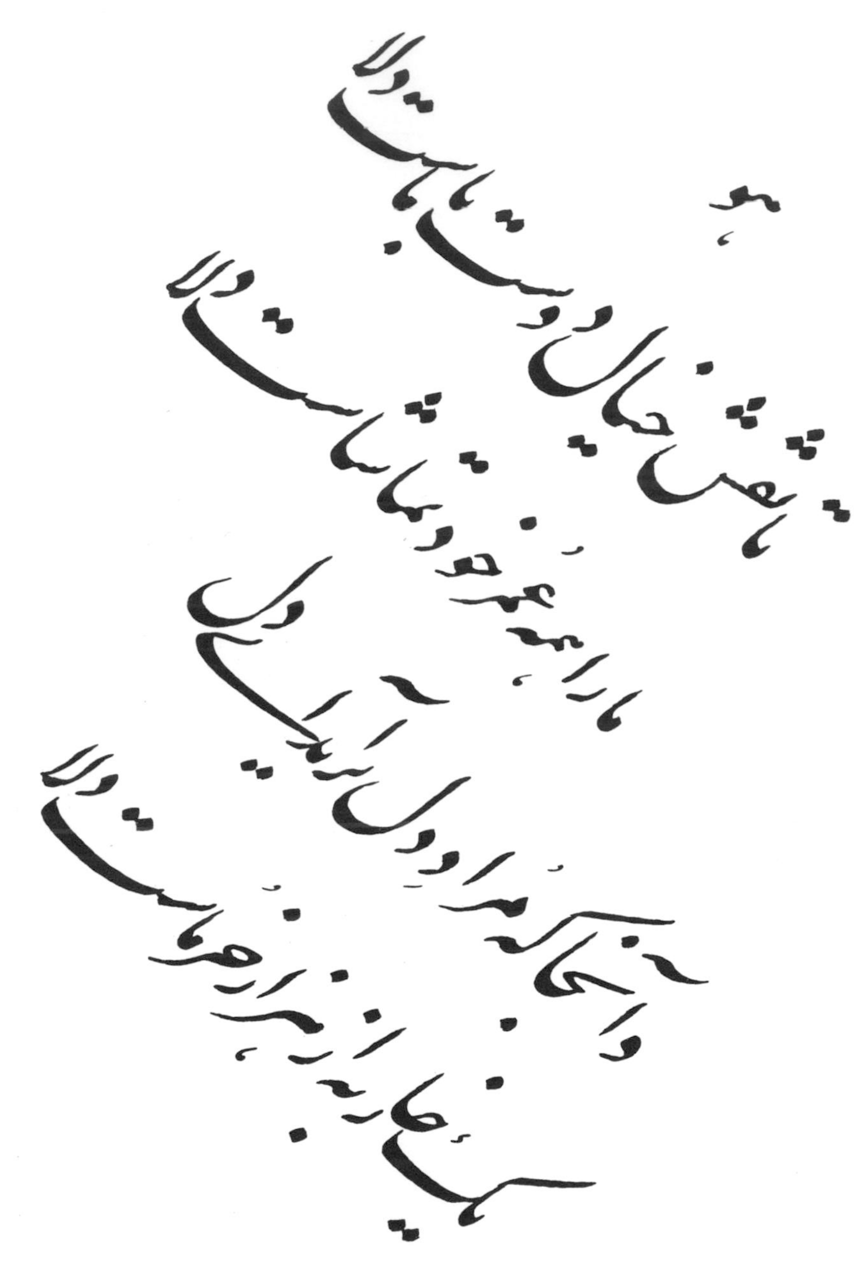

I could spend a lifetime
delighting in the image of the Friend.
But once my heart beholds the Friend,
then pain becomes more precious
than a thousand delights.

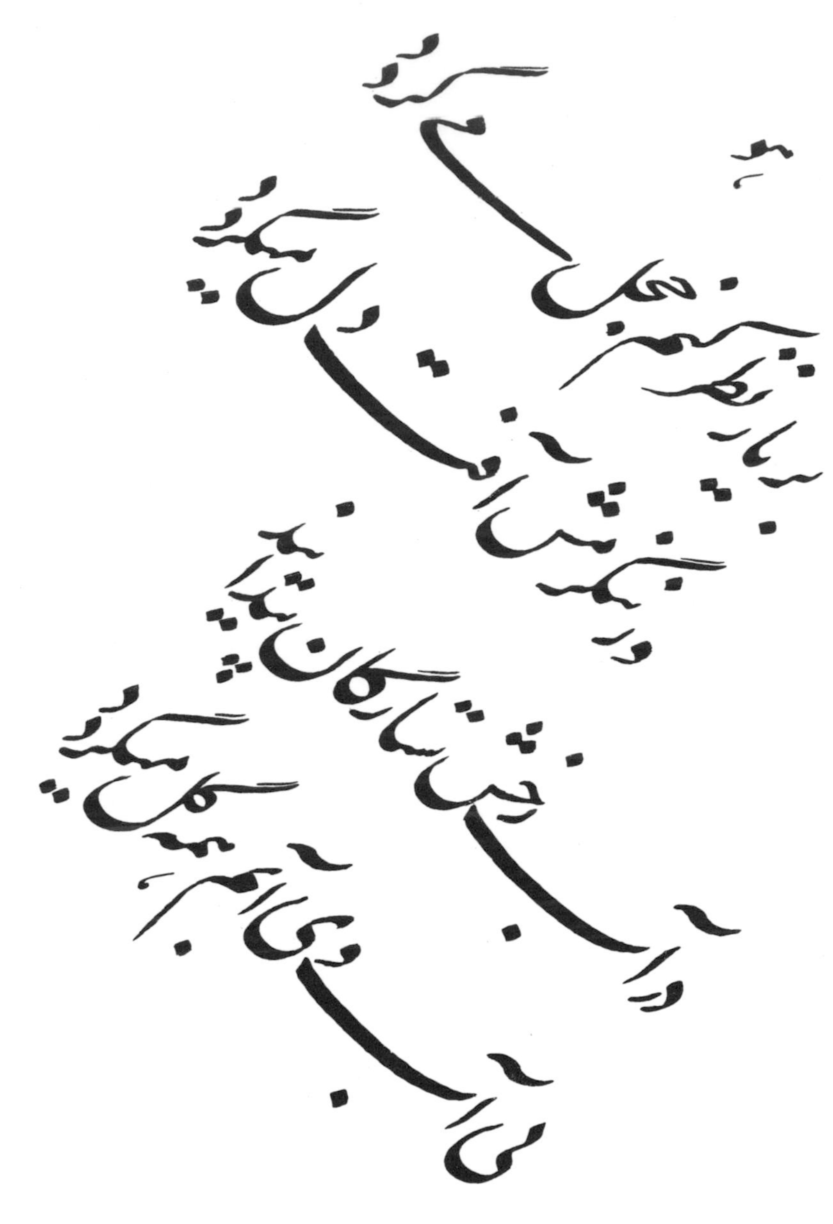

If I gaze at my beloved
she may feel embarrassed
and if I do not,
she will feel neglected.
I can see the stars reflecting
in the calm water of her face
but if I look away
I lose my clarity.

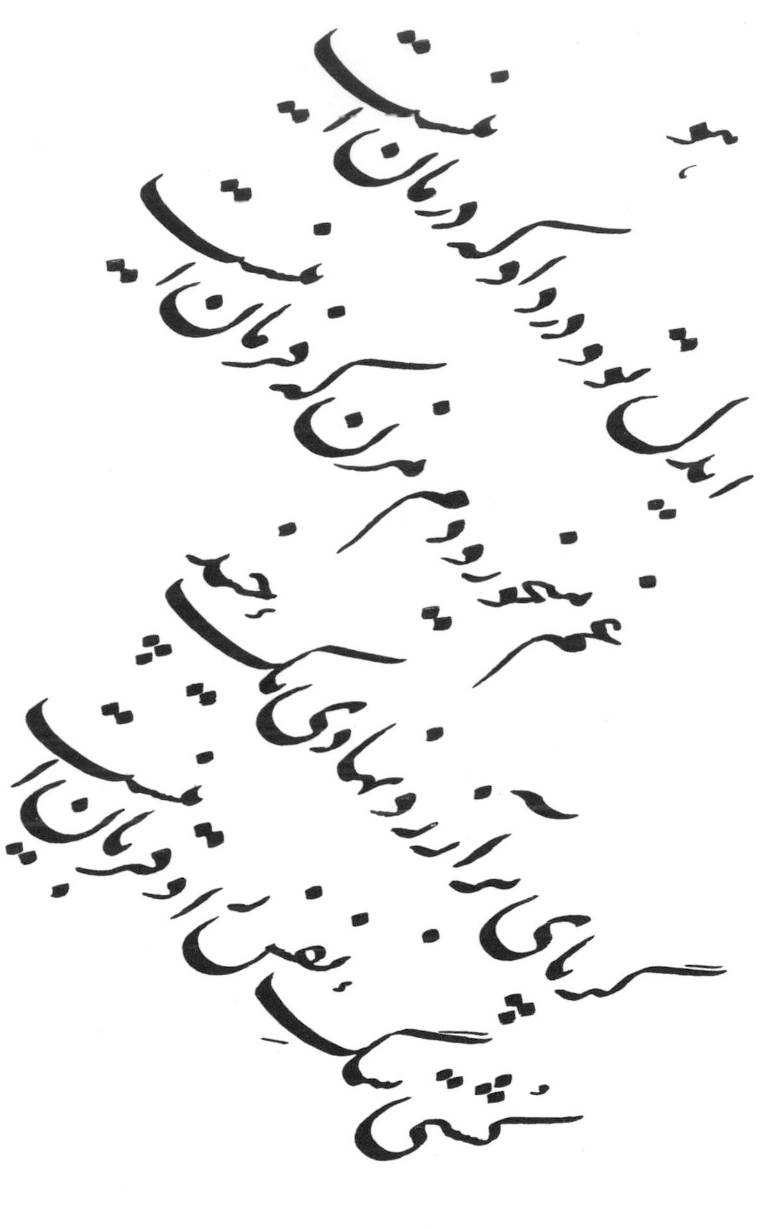
ای دل تو و درد او که درمان این است

Bear the pain of longing silently, my heart
for this is the cure.
The ultimate sacrifice is to curb your desires
and surrender the ego.

My body, like a cup, holds my heart
and my thoughts are like the young wine.
Knowledge is only a trap.
How do I know?
I received this message from the Heart.

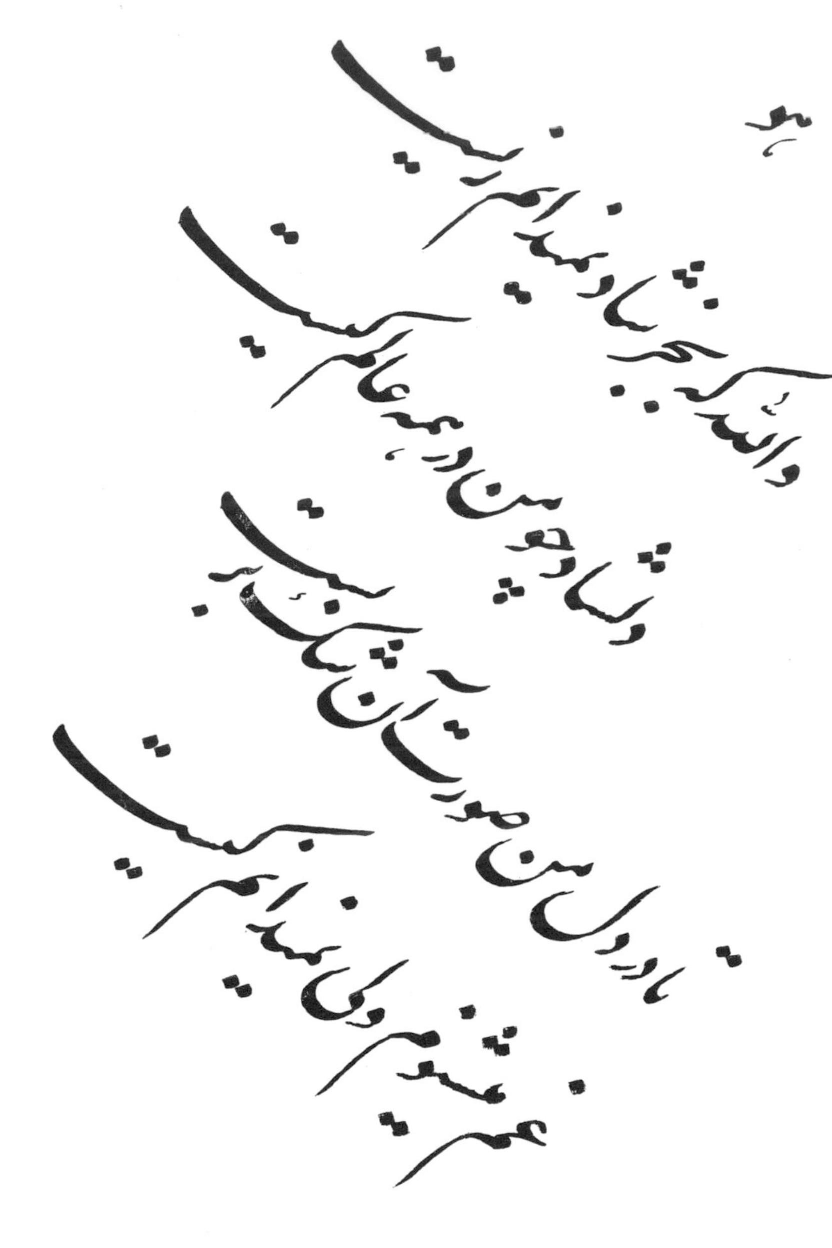

The treasure I hold in my heart
is the envy of all.
I swear to God
no one could be more joyous than me!
I hear about sorrow
but it means nothing to me.

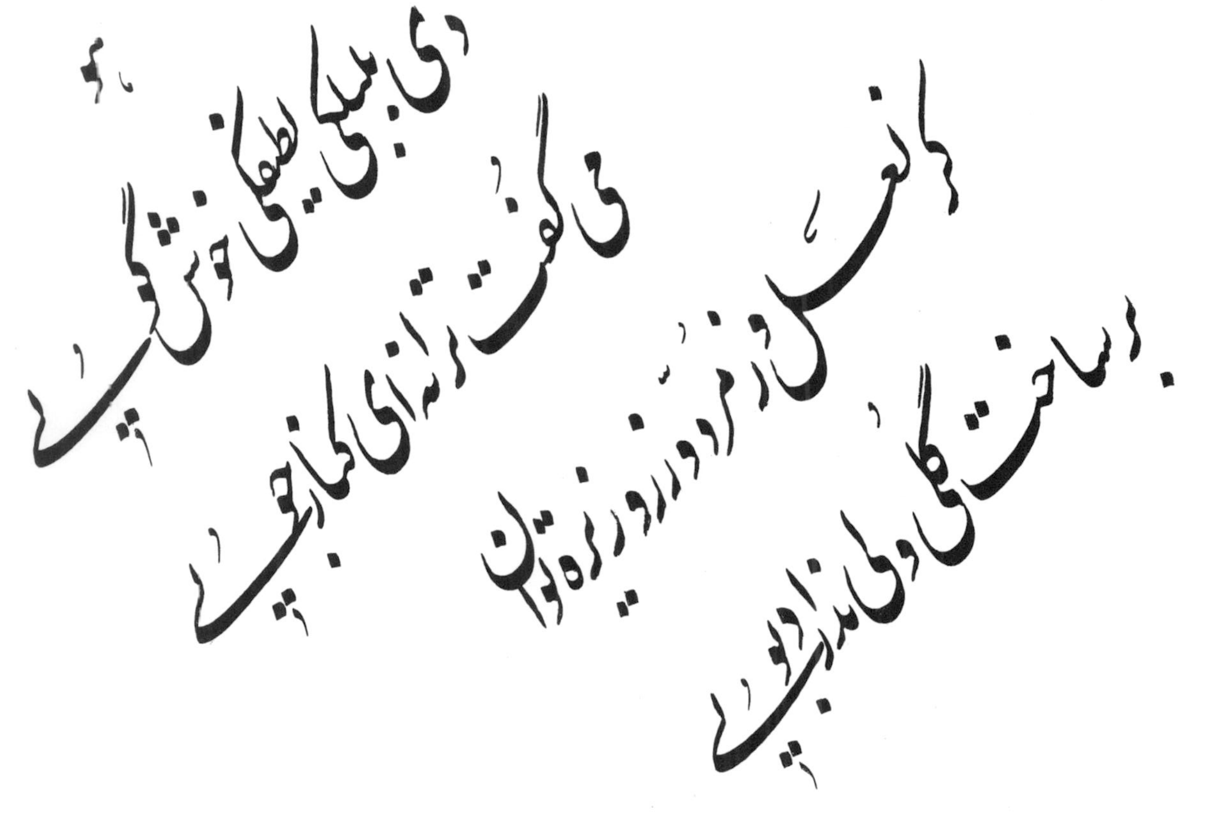
دی بلبلی لطیف خوش گوی
می گفت ترانه ای کنار جوی
بر ساخت گلی ولی ندارد بوی

Yesterday the nightingale was singing
a beautiful song by the stream:
"You could make a rose
out of rubies, emeralds and gold
but would it have a scent?"

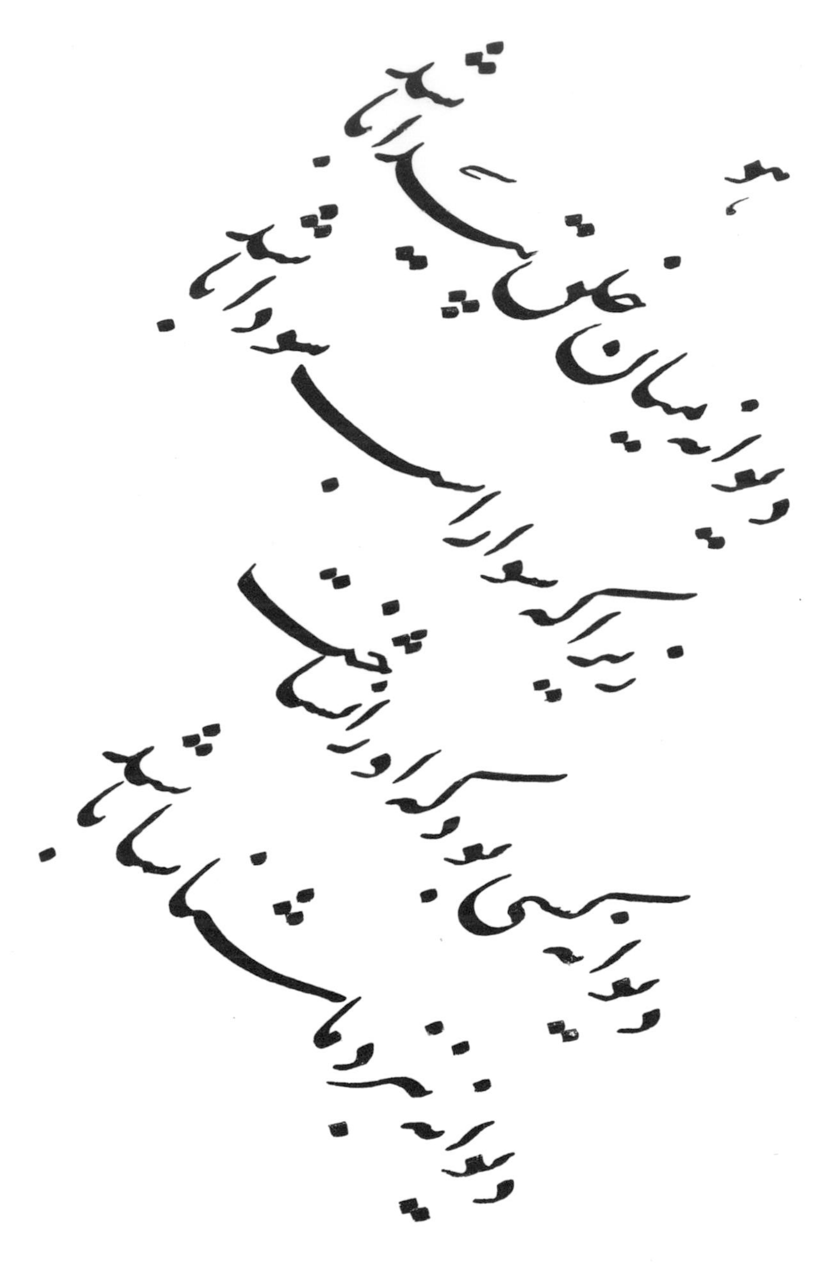

To the crowd
the dishevelled lover
riding on the horse of passion
is a madman.
But the truly mad ones
are those who are unable
to perceive him.

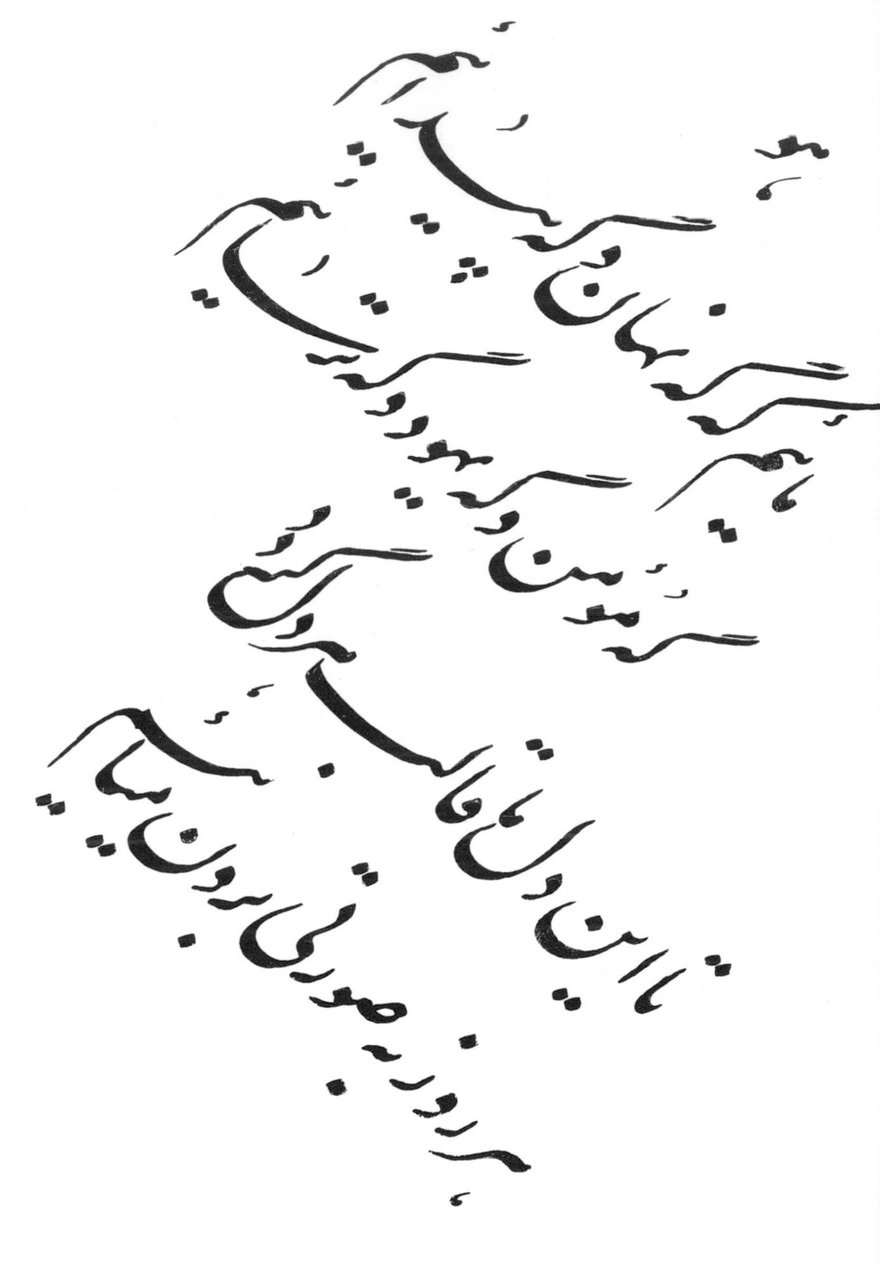

We may know who we are or we may not.
We may be Muslims, Jews or Christians
but until our hearts
become the mould for every heart
we will see only our differences.

I will not give up this pain so easily,
I will not give up this longing until I live.
Remembering Him is the sweetest pain
that I will not exchange for any cure.

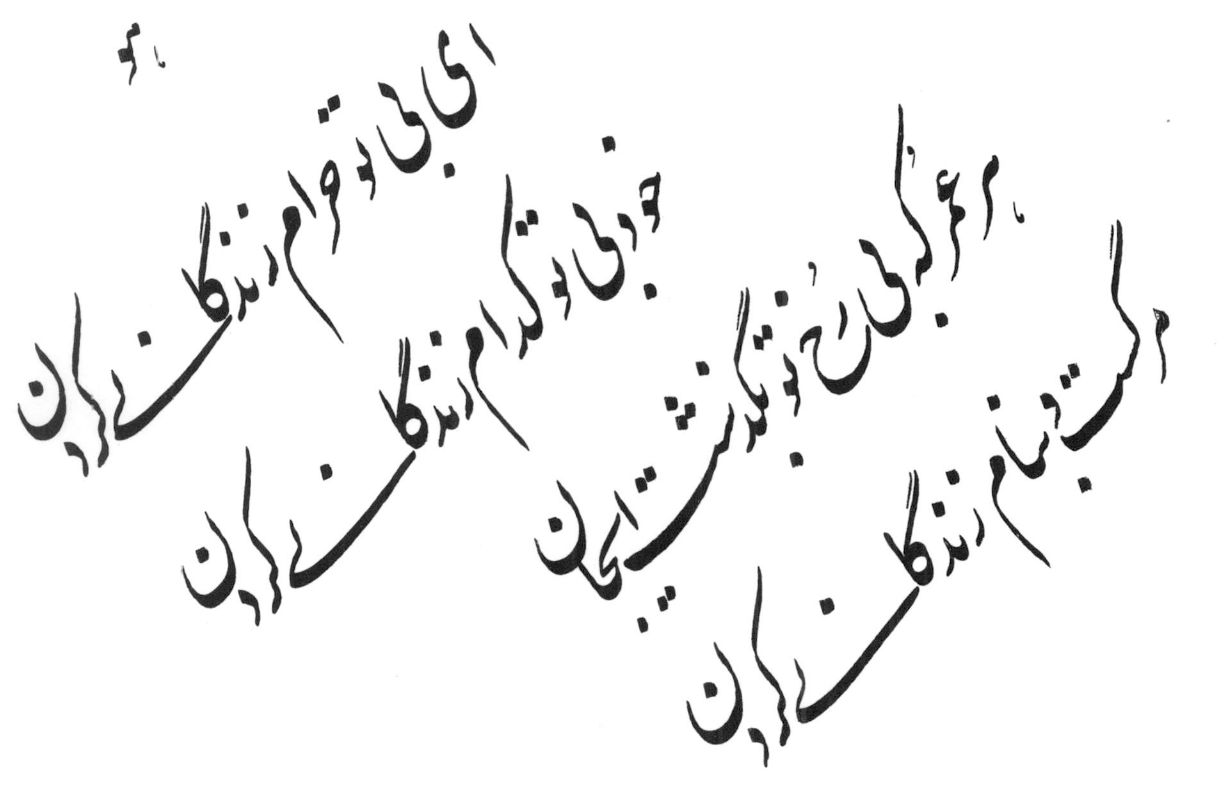
هو
ای بی تو حرام زندگانی کردن
چون بی تو کدام زندگانی کردن
هر عمر که بی رخ تو بگذشت ای جان
ننگست به نام زندگانی کردن

To live without you
is to be robbed of love
and what is life without it?
To live without you
is death to me, my love
but some call it life.

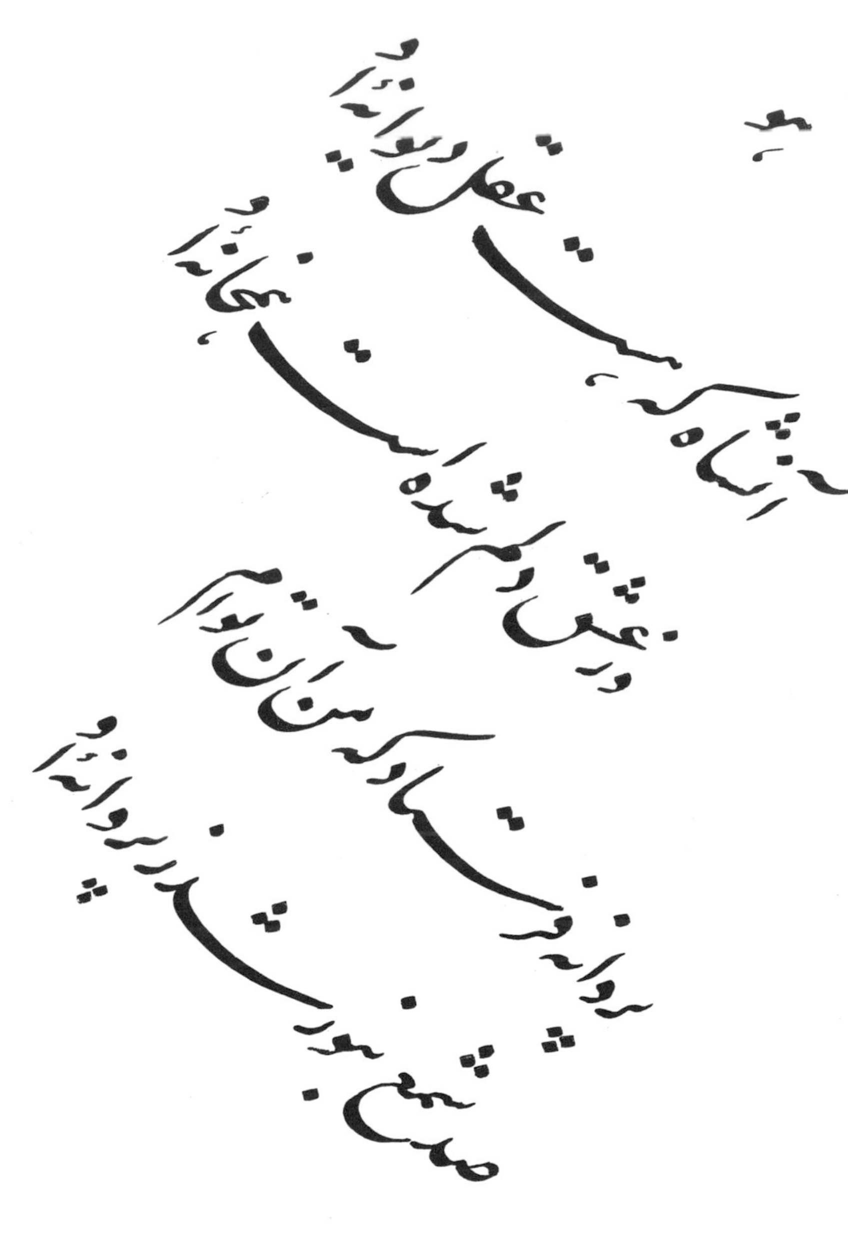

The King who stole my heart
sent a message with a butterfly.
It said, "I am yours"
and a hundred candles
burst into flame.

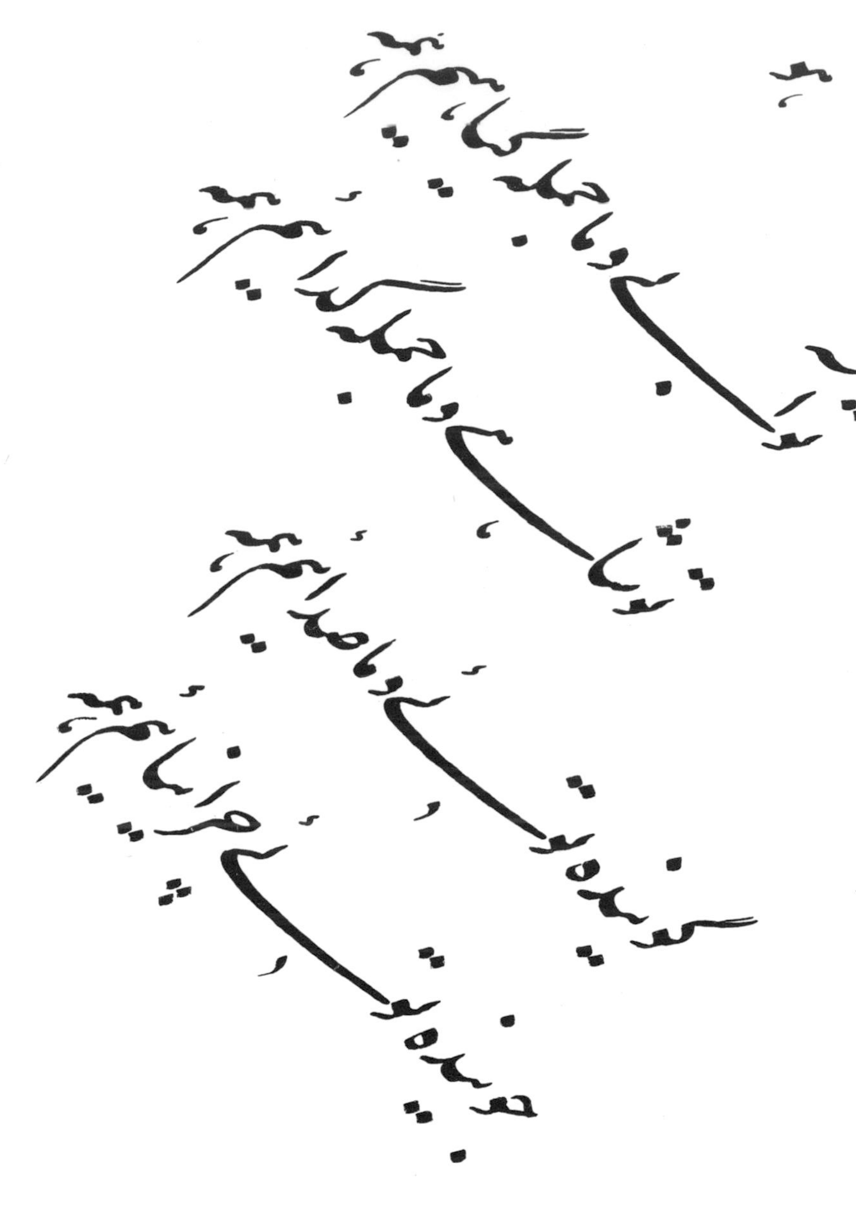

You are Water,
we are the thirsty plants,
You are the King,
we are the beggars at the gate,
You are the Speaker,
we are Your voice.
How could we not
answer Your call?

I want a lover with a fiery heart,
at war with the world and the stars;
a lover not afraid of bloodshed or murder,
and whose fire no water can quench.

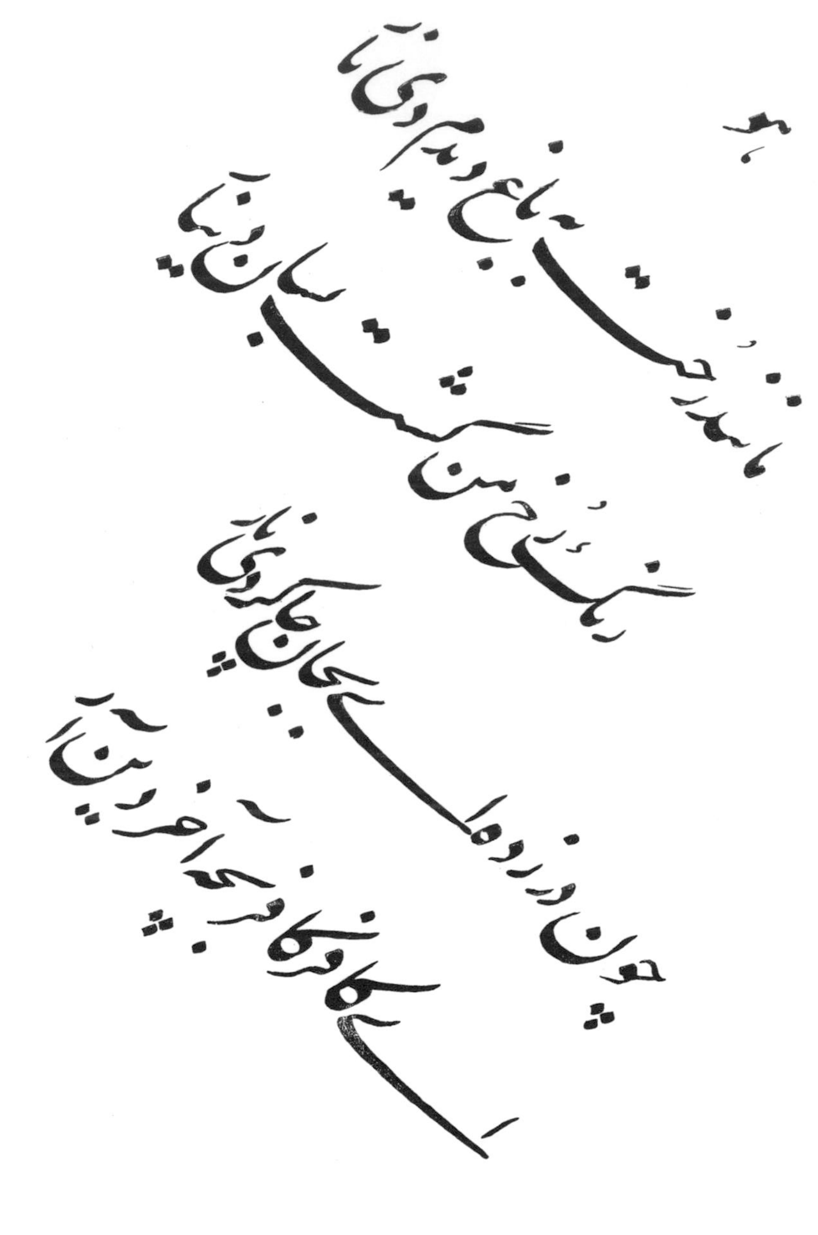

The pomegranate I saw yesterday
with the colour of your radiant face
set me on fire
and turned my face ashen and grey.
How do you expect me to trust you?

در انجمنی نشسته دیدم دوشش
نتوانستم گرفت در آغوشش
رخ را به بهانه بر رخش بنهادم
یعنی که حدیث میکنم در گوشش

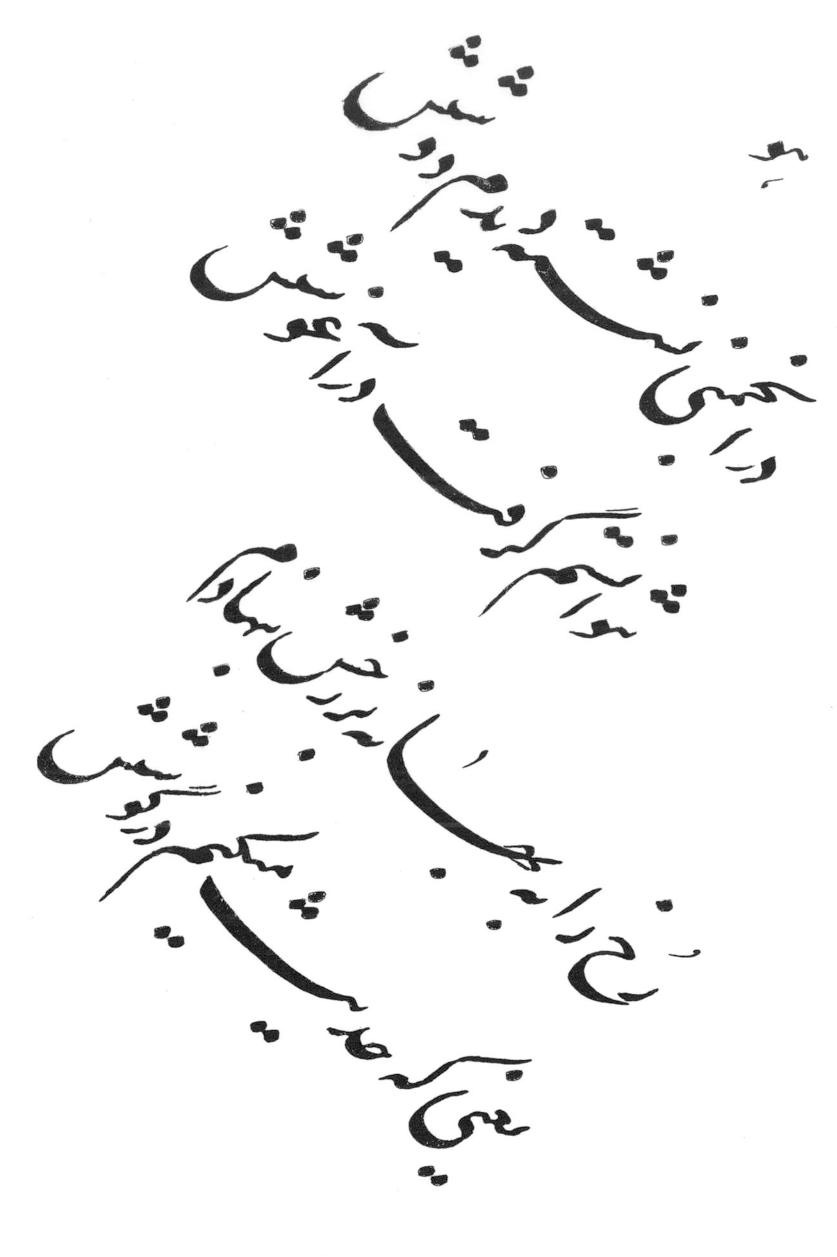

Last night in a gathering
I caught a glimpse of my beloved.
Too embarrassed to embrace him
I put my face against his cheek
pretending to whisper
something in his ear.

ما بیشتر از بهشت بیزاریم

در عین بهشت بی تو بیزاریم

گر جمله جهان بهشت گلستان تو

بی دامن دوست از بهشت بیزاریم

Never lose hope, my heart,
miracles dwell in the invisible.
If the whole world turns against you
keep your eyes on the Friend.

هو

اندیشه مکن مکن تو خود را ز حجاب
کاندیشه ز روی مه سحاب است حجاب
دل چون ماه است تو در دل اندیشه‌ها
اندر اندیشه نگیری از آب

Put your thoughts to sleep,
do not let them cast a shadow
over the moon of your heart.
Let go of thinking.

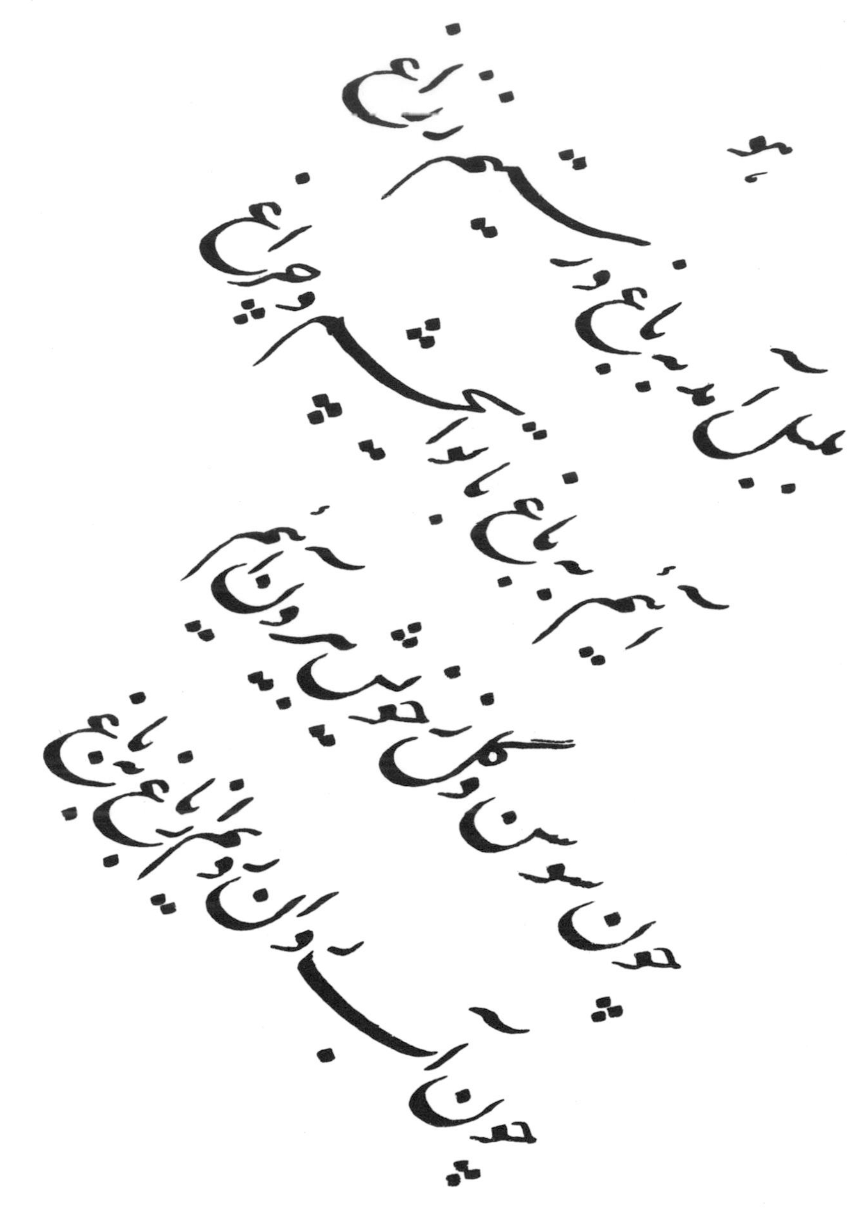

Light of my eyes
the nightingale has returned.
We will lose ourselves in the garden
and come out in blossom
like the lilies and roses;
we will become water and flow
from garden to garden.

I am whirled into ecstasy!
The drunken nightingale sings in my ear.
I hear your luring voice in the wind,
your image sparkles on the water,
the delicate scent in the air
is so familiar . . .

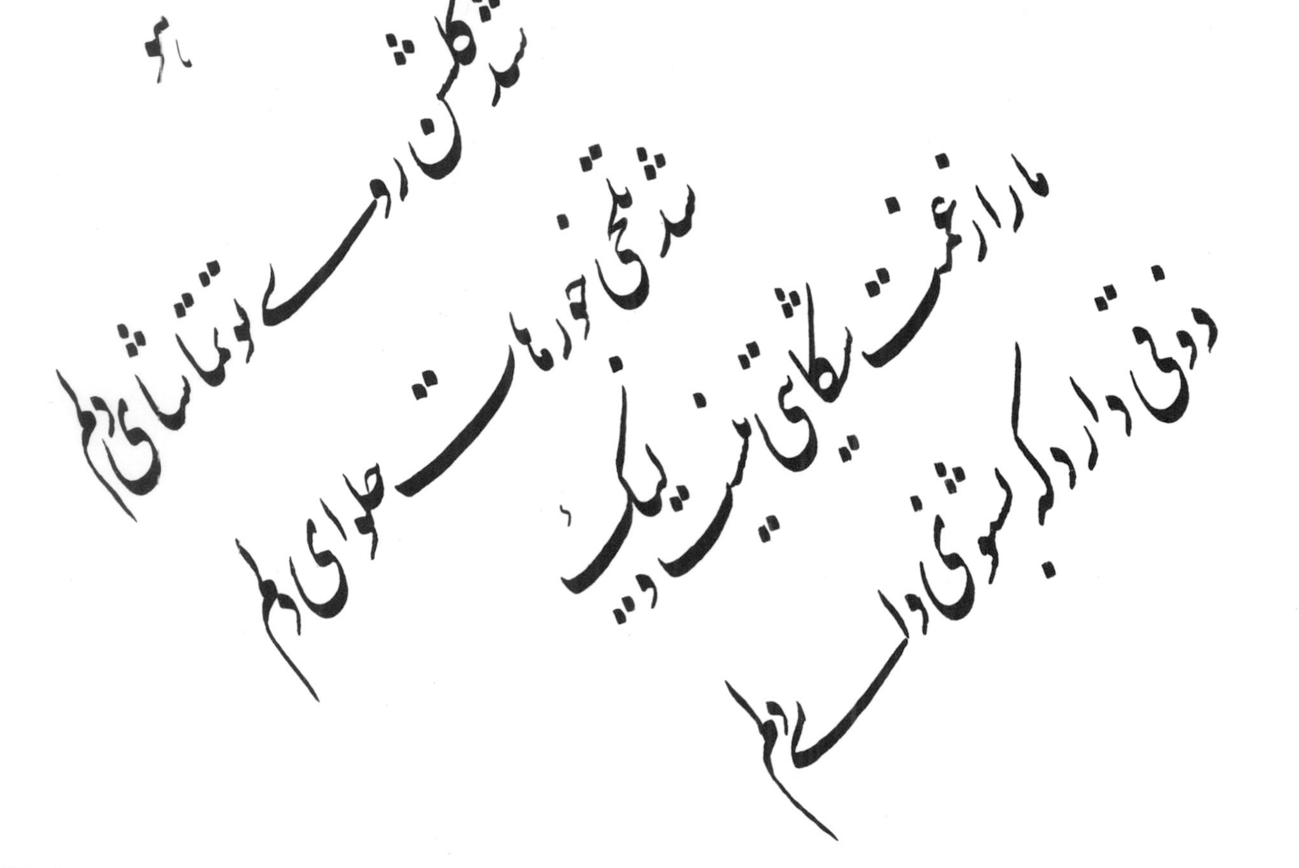
شد گلشن روی تو تماشای دلم
شد تلخی جورهات حلوای دلم
ما را ز غمت شکایتی نیست ولی

Is your face a beautiful blossom

or a sweet torture?

I have no complaints

but my heart is tempted

to let you

hear of its sorrows.

هو

من بی‌غم غم خدای خود نماید
کاندر دل من مرا چه حاجت آید
باری دل من شاخ گل زاید
کز باد صبا به لطف می‌افشاید

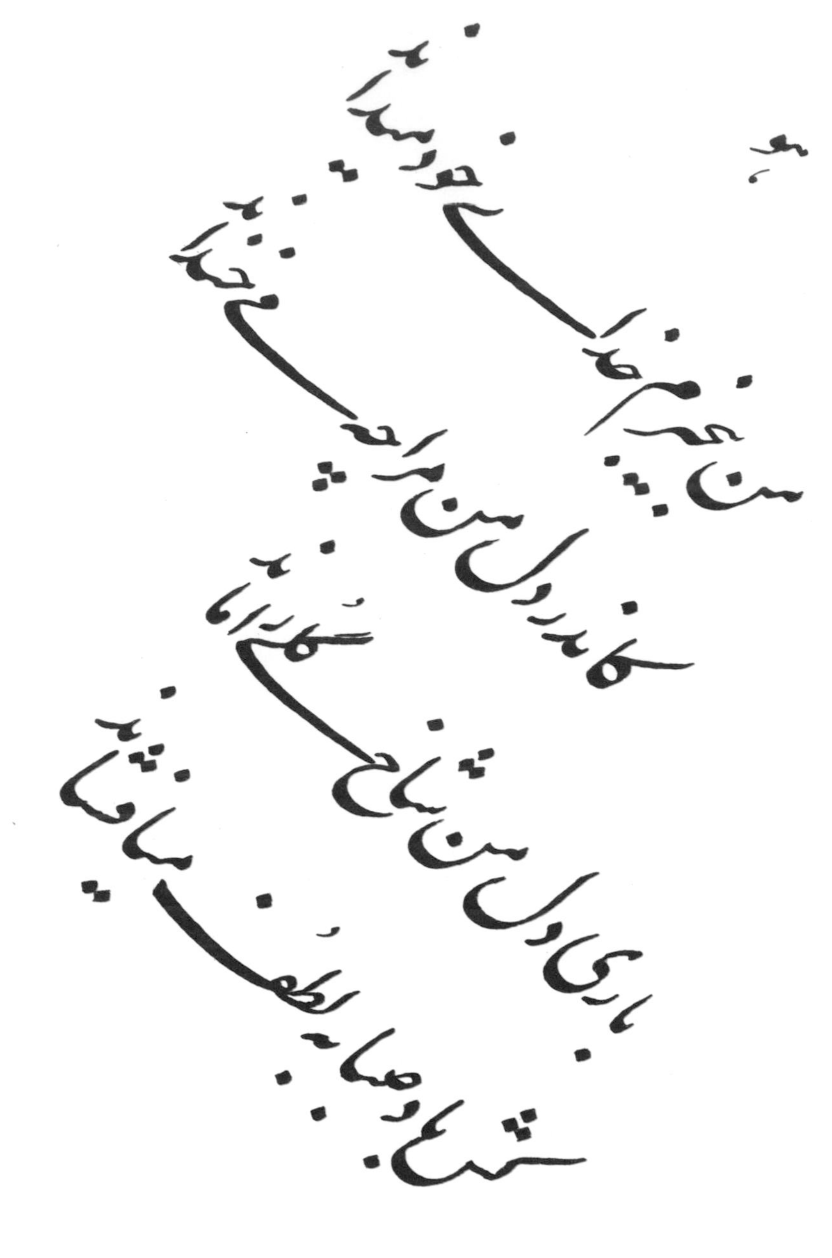

God only knows
what this joy, this laughter
bubbling inside my heart, could be!
Maybe the playful wind is scattering
the rose petals of my heart.

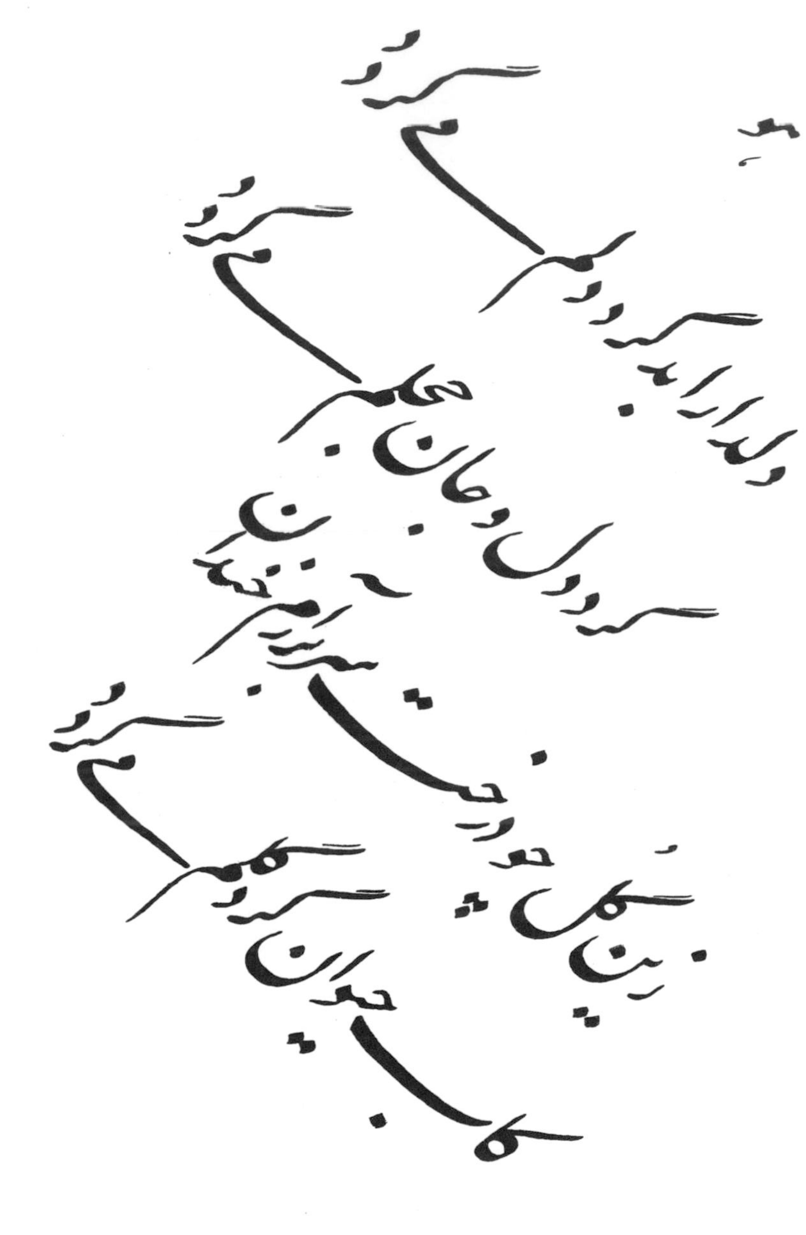

Eternal Love turns incessantly
around my humbled heart
and, smiling,
I will rise from the ground
like a tree
because the water of life
turns incessantly
around me.

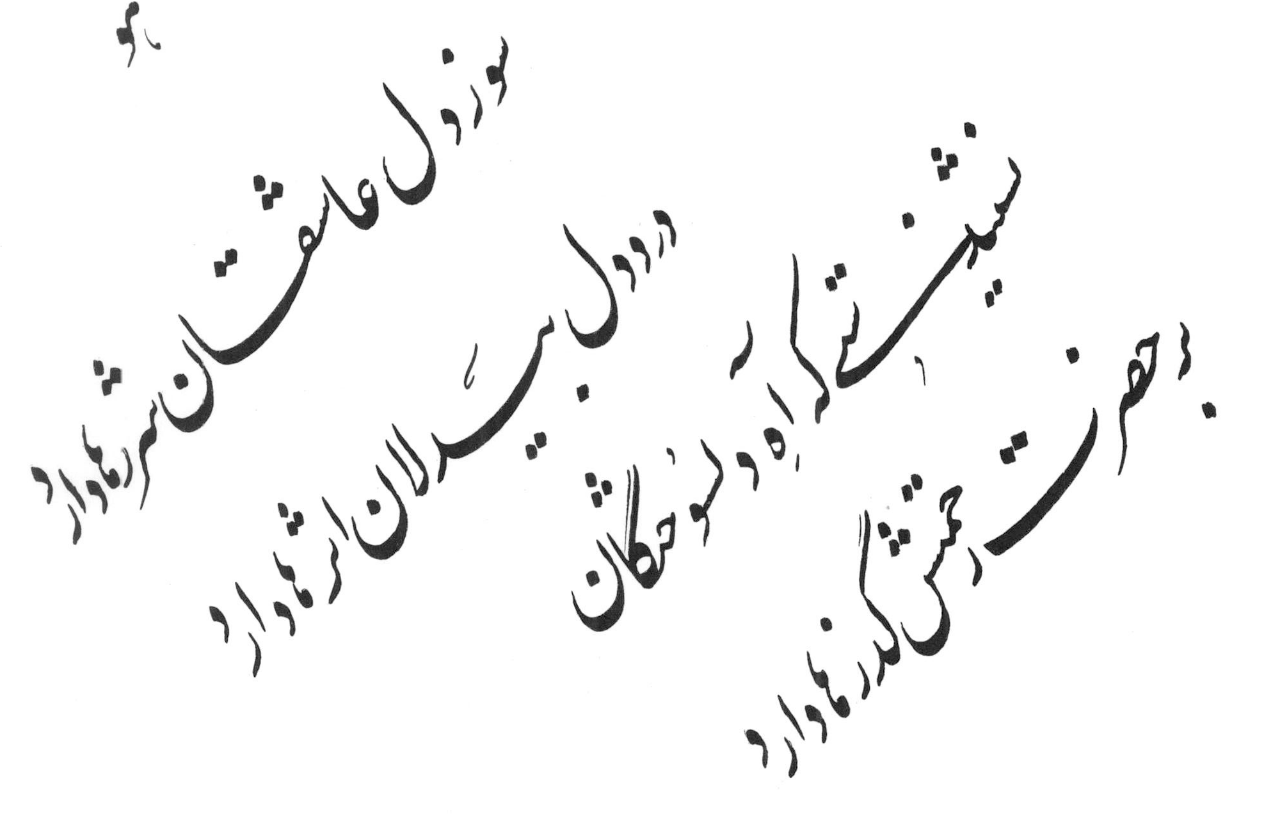
هو
سوز دل عاشقان شررها دارد
درد دل بیدلان اثرها دارد
نشنیده‌ای که آه دلسوختگان
بر حضرت رحمتش گذرها دارد

A special spark rises
from the sorrow of a burning heart.
Have you ever heard
how the sigh of a broken heart
touches the Beloved?

هو

شادم که غم تو در دل من گنجد

زیرا که غمت به جای روشن گنجد

آن غم که نگنجد در افلاک و زمین

اندر دل چون چشمهٔ سوزن گنجد

I am delighted
that my heart welcomes sorrow
for the sorrow
that the earth and the sky
can not behold
is contained in a heart
as small
as the eye of a needle.

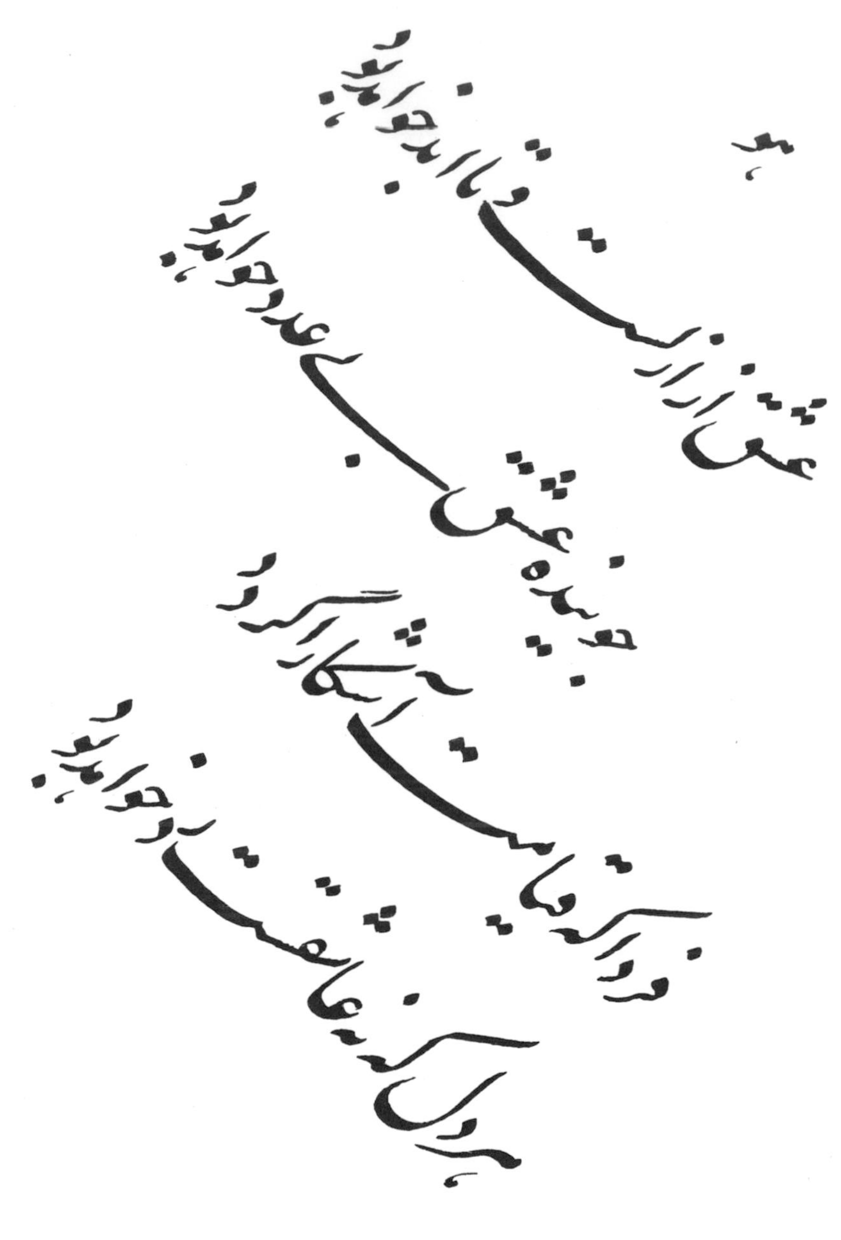

Love was from the beginning of time
and love will be for all eternity.
On the day of resurrection
the heart devoid of love will not pass
through the gate.

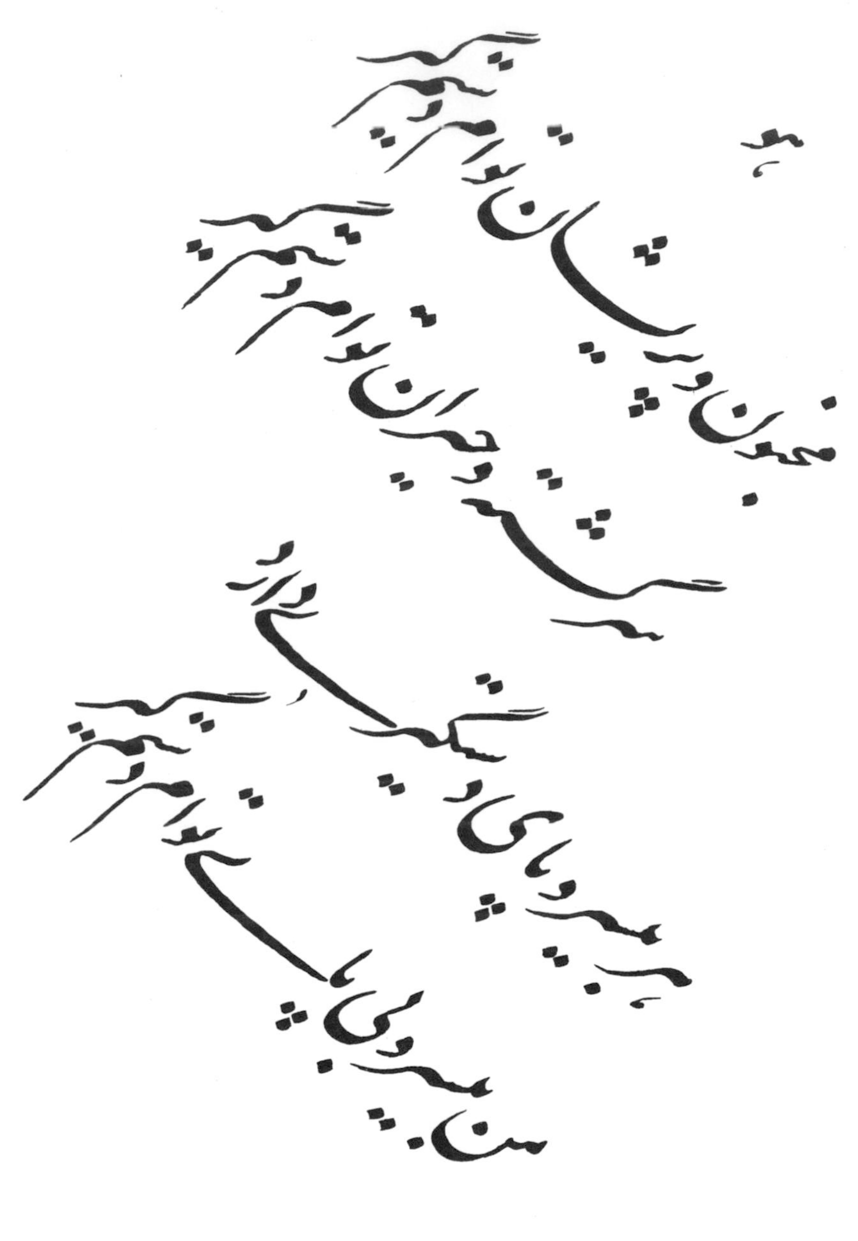

I have become insane and bewildered,

take my hand.

Even the most unworthy have a friend,

I am lost without You.

Take my hand!

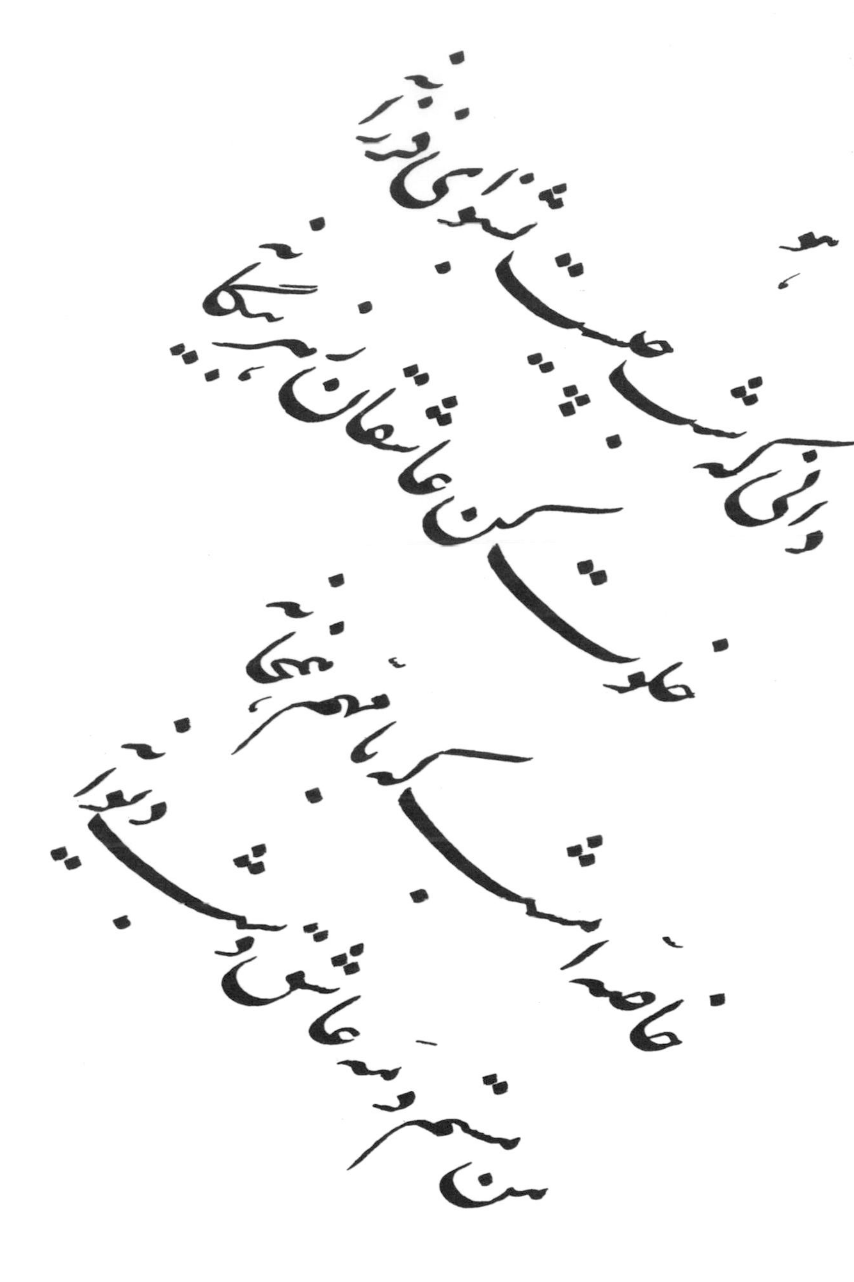

Do you know, knower,

what the night is?

It is the sanctuary of lovers.

On this glorious night

I am drunk with the moon.

The moon has fallen in love

and the night has gone mad.

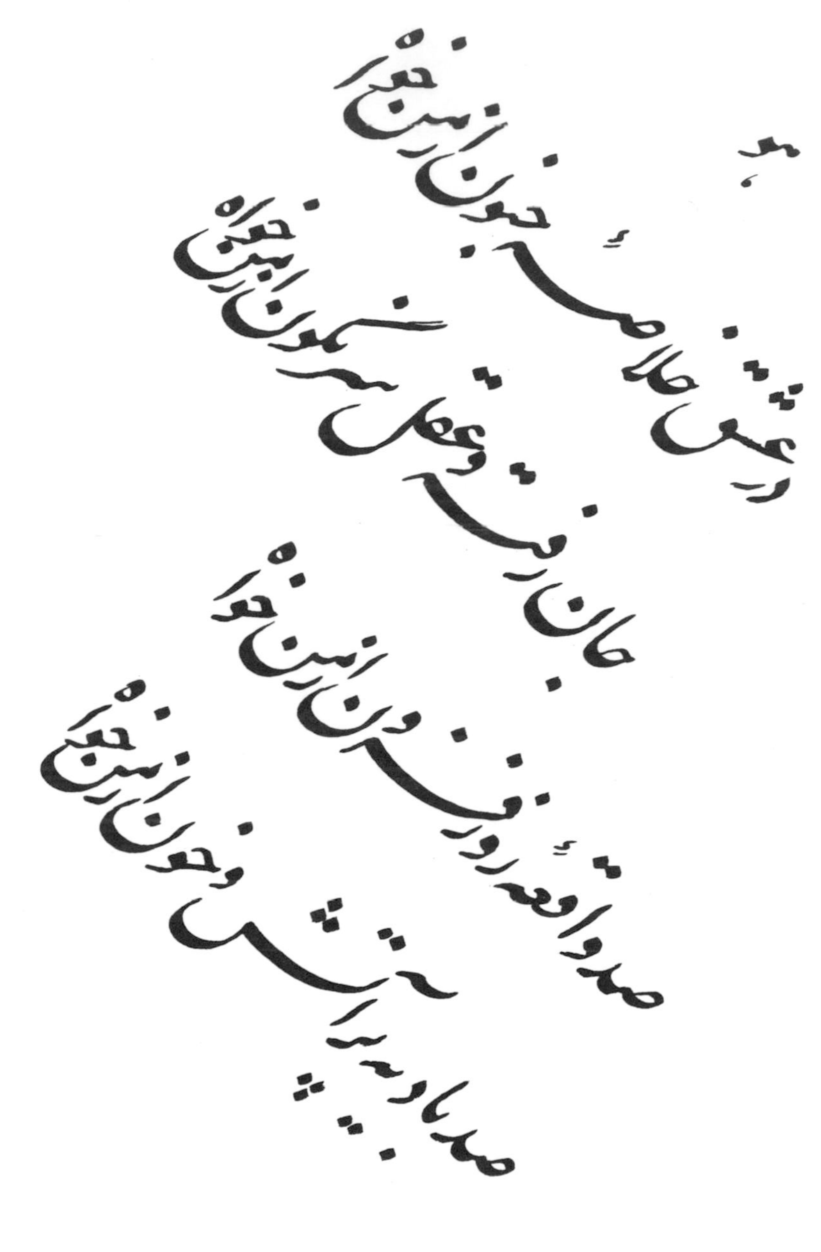

In love, ask for madness,
a life abandoned and a mind lost,
ask for dangerous adventures
in deserts filled with blood and fire!

Hesitate

and I will tear apart your patience.

Fall asleep

and I will snatch the sleep from your eyes.

Become a mountain

and I will set it on fire

Become an ocean

and I will drink all its water.

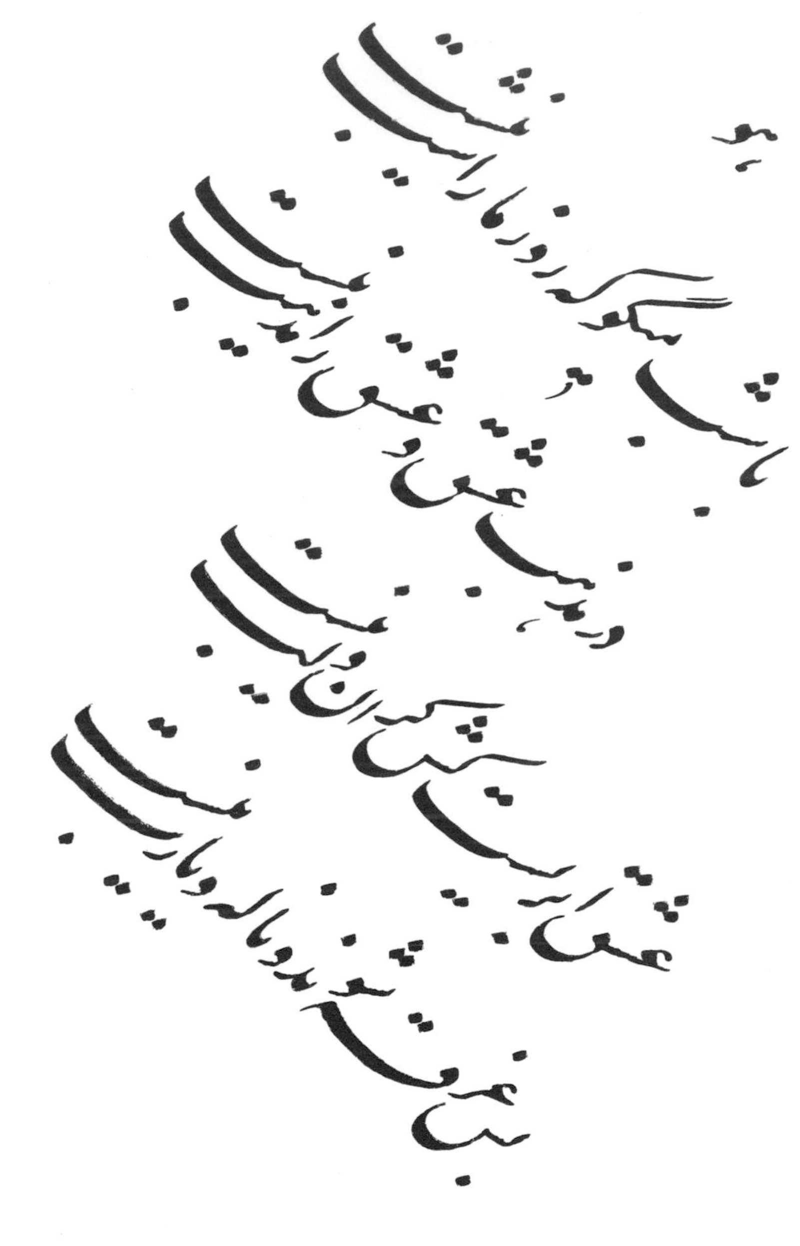

Lover, tell the night
that your day
will never end in its arms.
The religion of Love
is a sea without a shore
where lovers drown
without a sigh,
without a cry.

با روی تو هیچ کس ز باغ اندیشد
با عشق تو از شمع و چراغ اندیشد
گویند که وقت است دماغ از خوابست
عاشق نشود کسی که از دماغ اندیشد

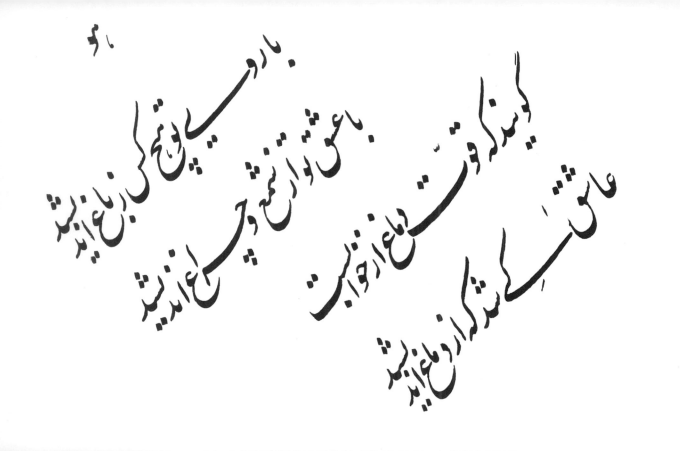

Would I think of gardens, beloved,
with your face by my side?
Would I long for light, beloved,
when I am lit by the fire of your love?
They say sleep strengthens the mind
but does a lover need a mind?

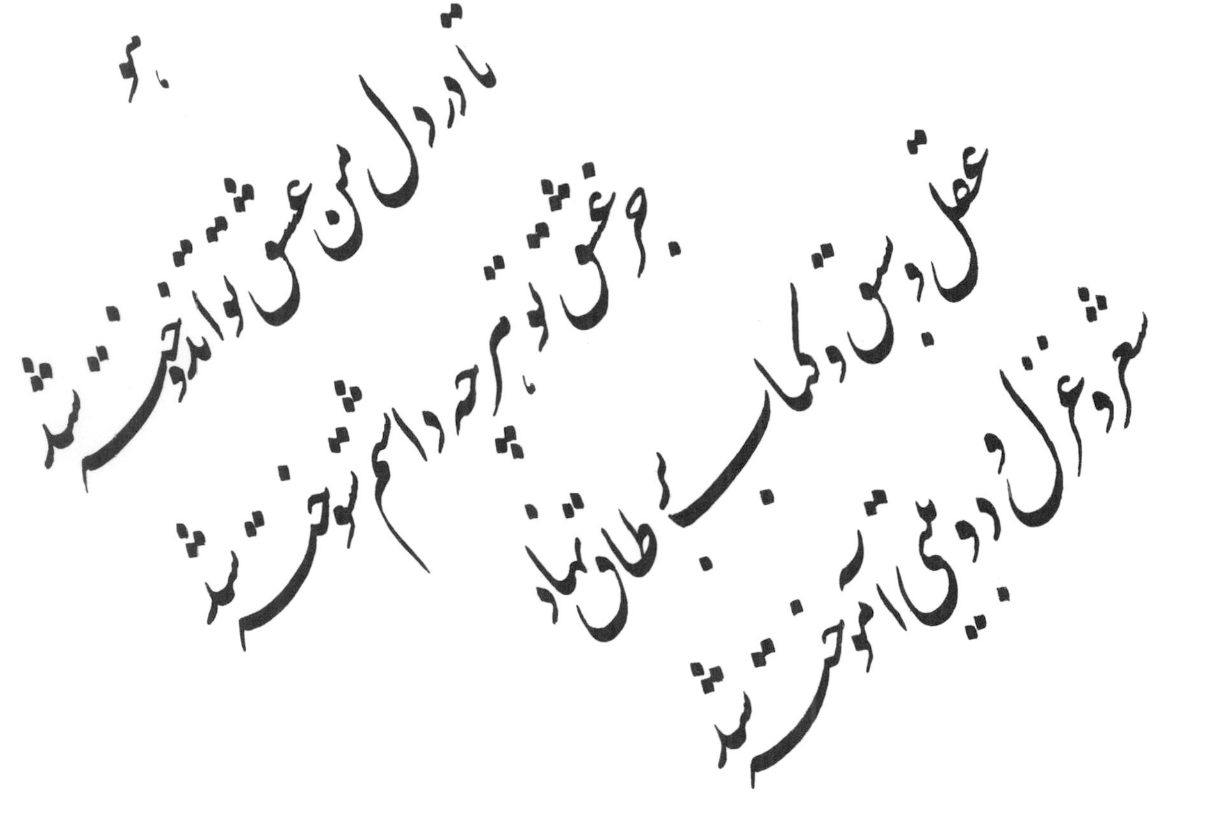
هو
تا در دل من عشق تو اندوخته شد
جز عشق تو هر چه داشتم سوخته شد
عقل و سبق و کتاب بر طاق نهاد
شعر و غزل و دوبیتی آموخته شد

The fire of Love blazed in my heart
and consumed everything.
My books, my erudition and my mind
I put away on a shelf.
Now I only write poems.

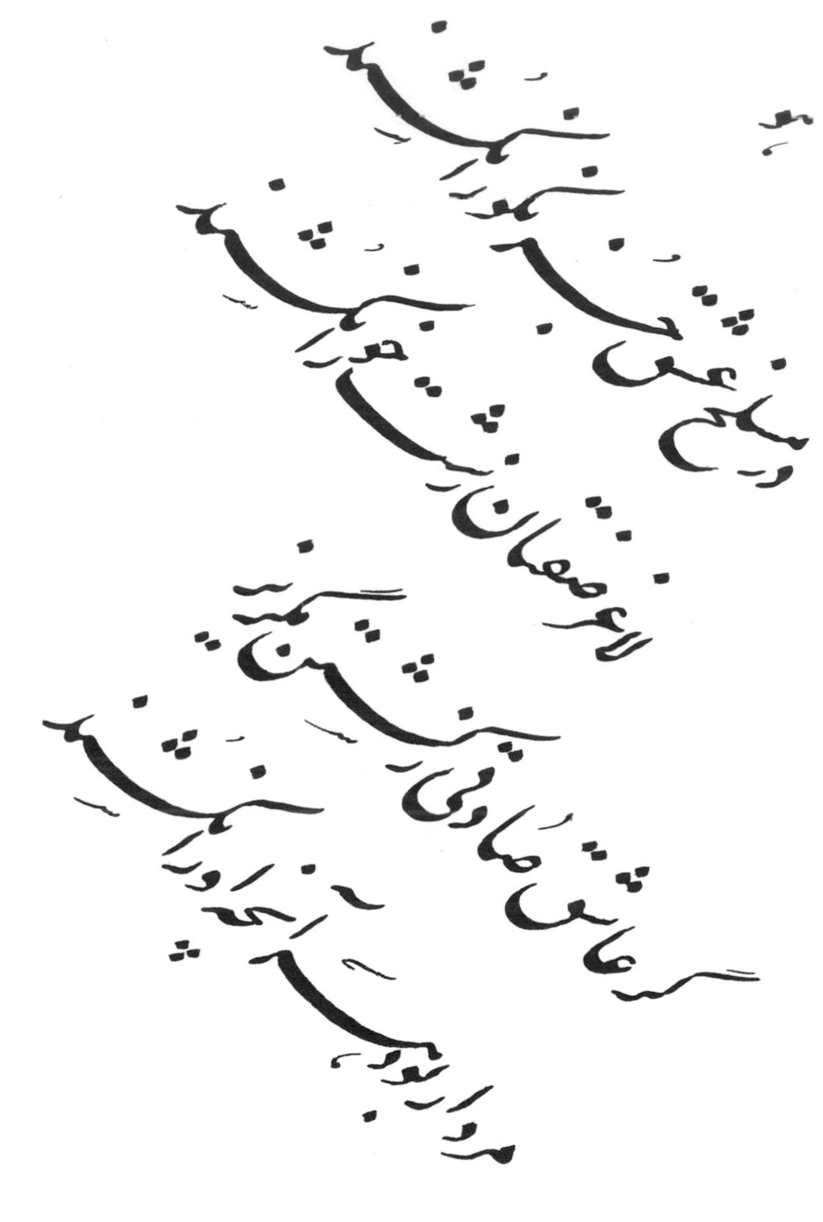

In the kitchen of love
only the beautiful are killed.
Death does not frighten a true lover
for those not dying for love
are already corpses.

گر شائقی به پیش مشتاق نشین
روزان و شبان بر عشاق نشین
آنگاه چو این حلقه گسستی گهی
از خلق گذر کن بر خلاق نشین

When you are taken by Love
sit day and night
at the door of the enchanted lovers.
Once you have unlocked
the mystery in their circle
you may pass beyond the created
and sit at the door of the Creator.

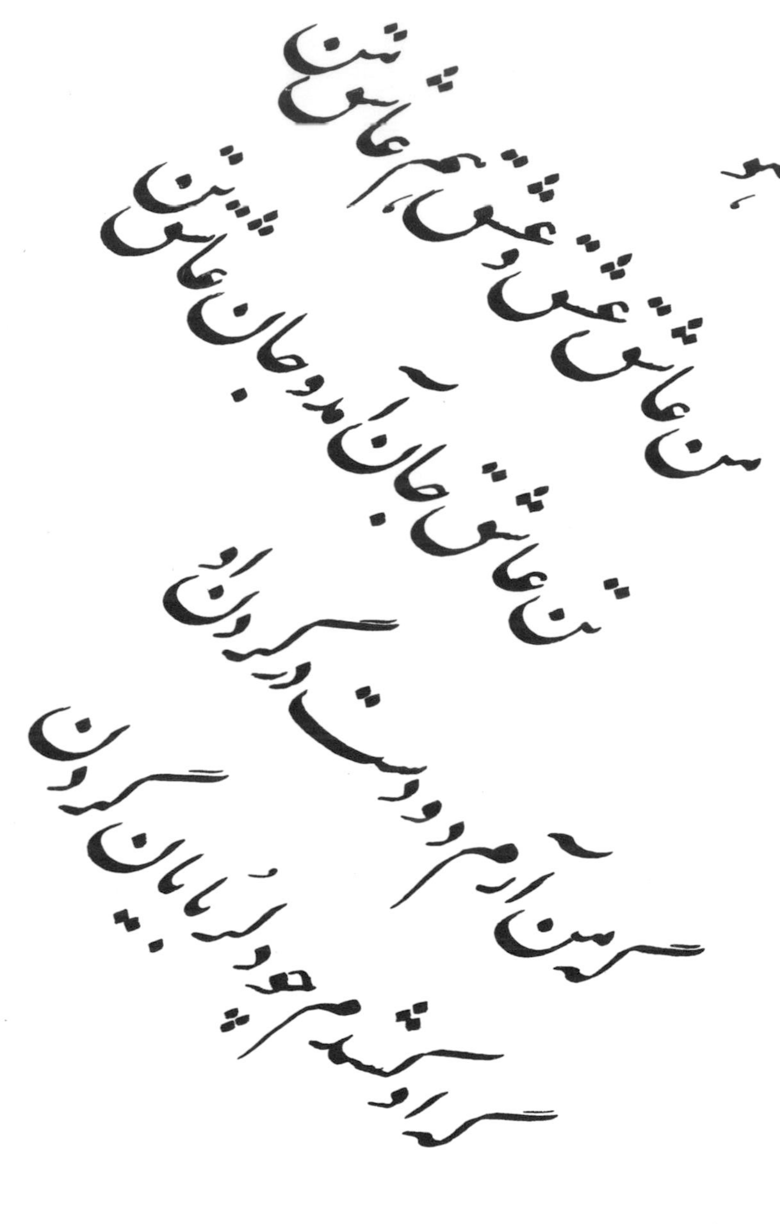
هو
من عاشق عشق و عشق هم عاشق من
تن عاشق جان آمد و جان عاشق تن

I am in love with Love and Love
is in love with me.
My body is in love with the soul
and the soul
is in love with my body.
I opened my arms to Love
and Love embraced me
like a lover.

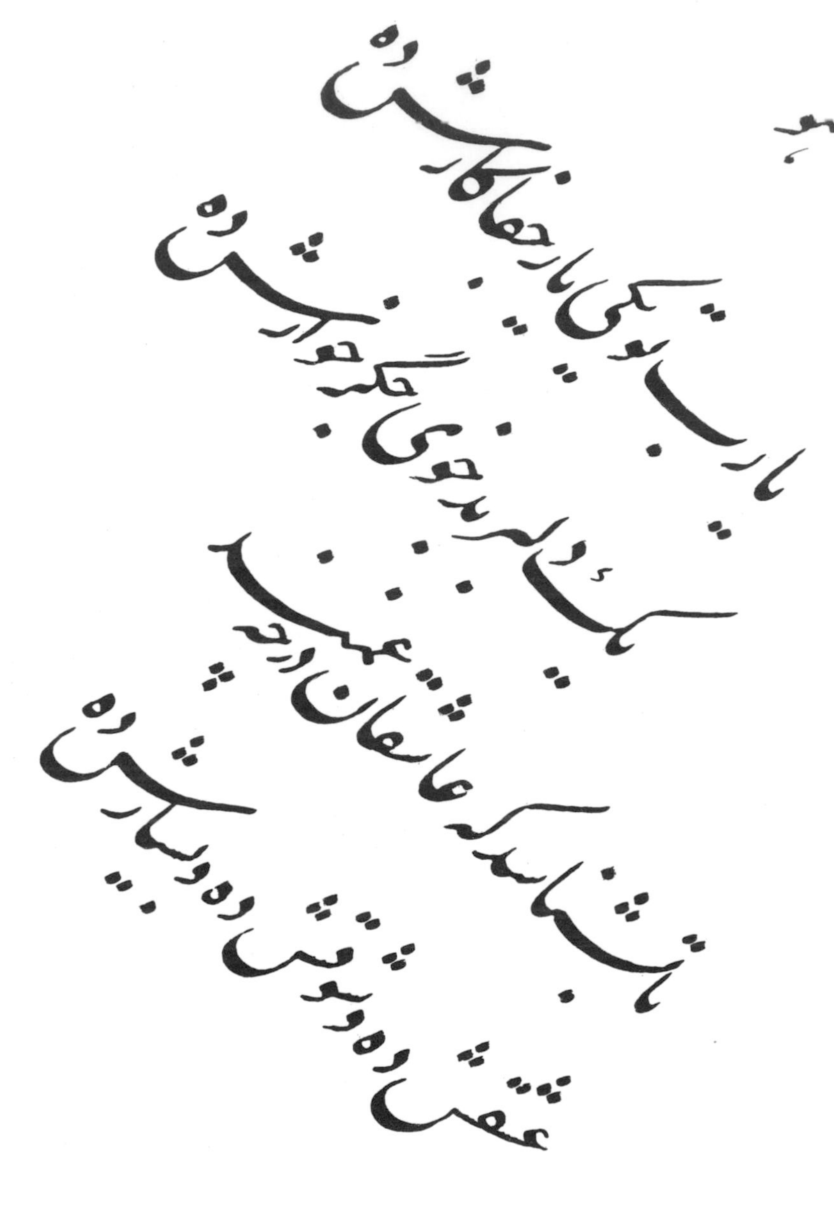

Oh God, give them a cruel lover,
let them be consumed with passion
for someone ill-tempered and bloodthirsty
so that they know the pain a true lover feels!

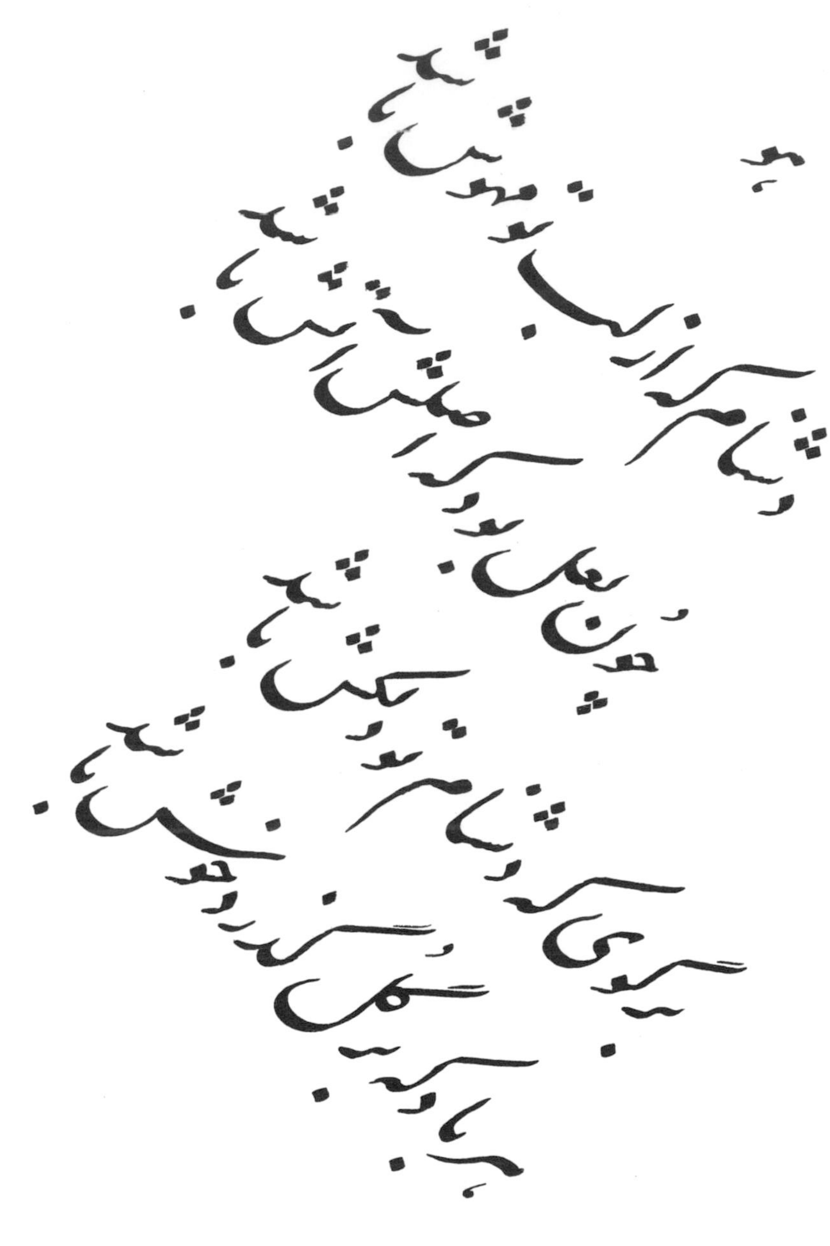

From your lips
scorn is as beautiful as the ruby
holding fire in its essence.
From your lips
scorn is as gentle as the breeze
caressing the flowers.

هو

یاری کن و یار باش ای یار عجب

ای بلبل سرمست به گلزار عجب

یاران عزیز را نگهدار عجب

امشب بخشش است زنهار عجب

Do not desert me,

be my friend, my help, beloved.

Be my enchanting nightingale, my garden.

Do not abandon your lonely friend.

Tonight the night is generous and merciful,

do not desert me!

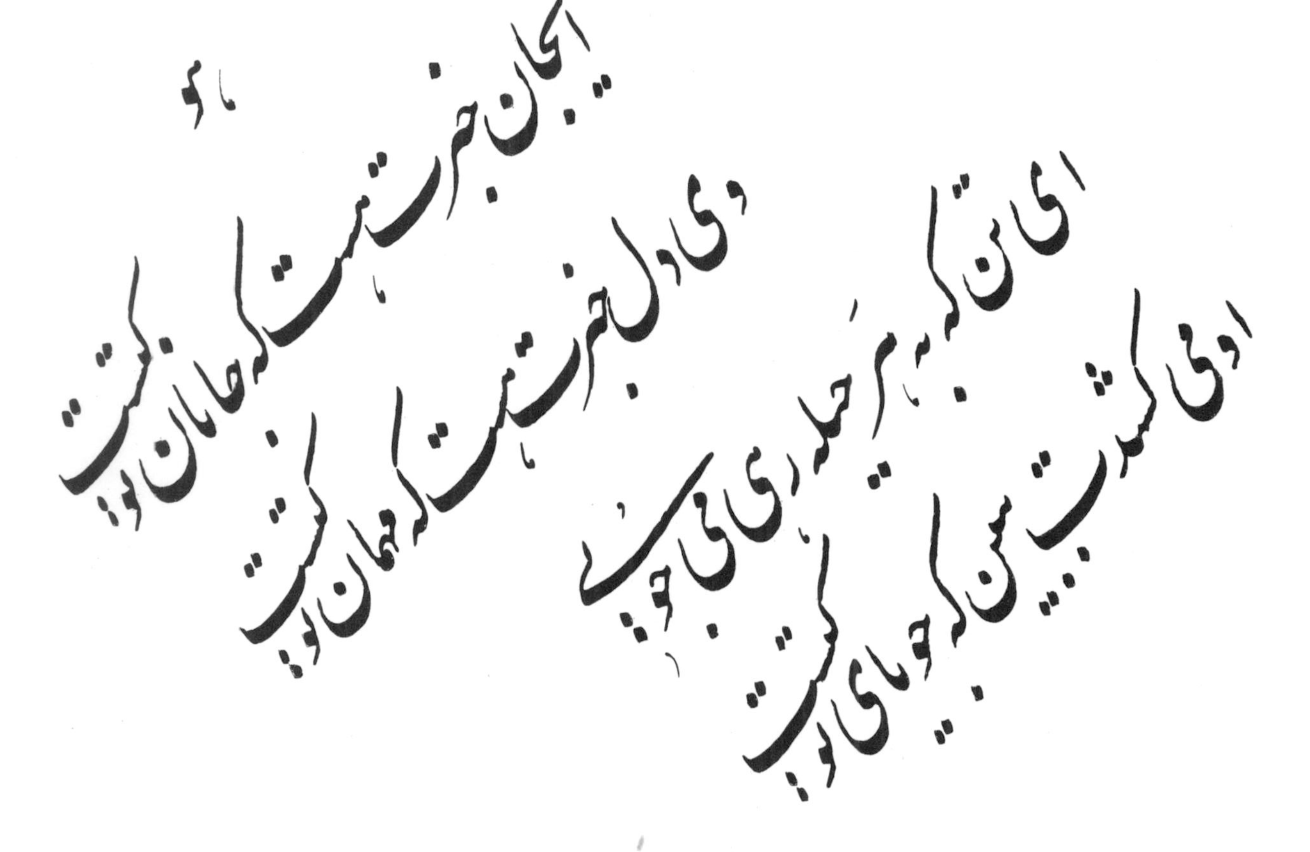
ای جان جز این نیست که جانان تو کیست
وی دل جز این نیست که مهمان تو کیست
ای تن که به هر حیله رهی می‌جویی
وی کشته بی‌سمن که جوهای تو کیست

My spirit

know and behold the eternal Spirit.

My heart

know and honour your Guest.

My body

know that no trick will save you from

the One

who seeks you.

I know that my spirit belongs
to the Spirit of all Spirit.
I know I belong to the city
of those who have no place.
But to find my way there
I need to let go of my knowing.

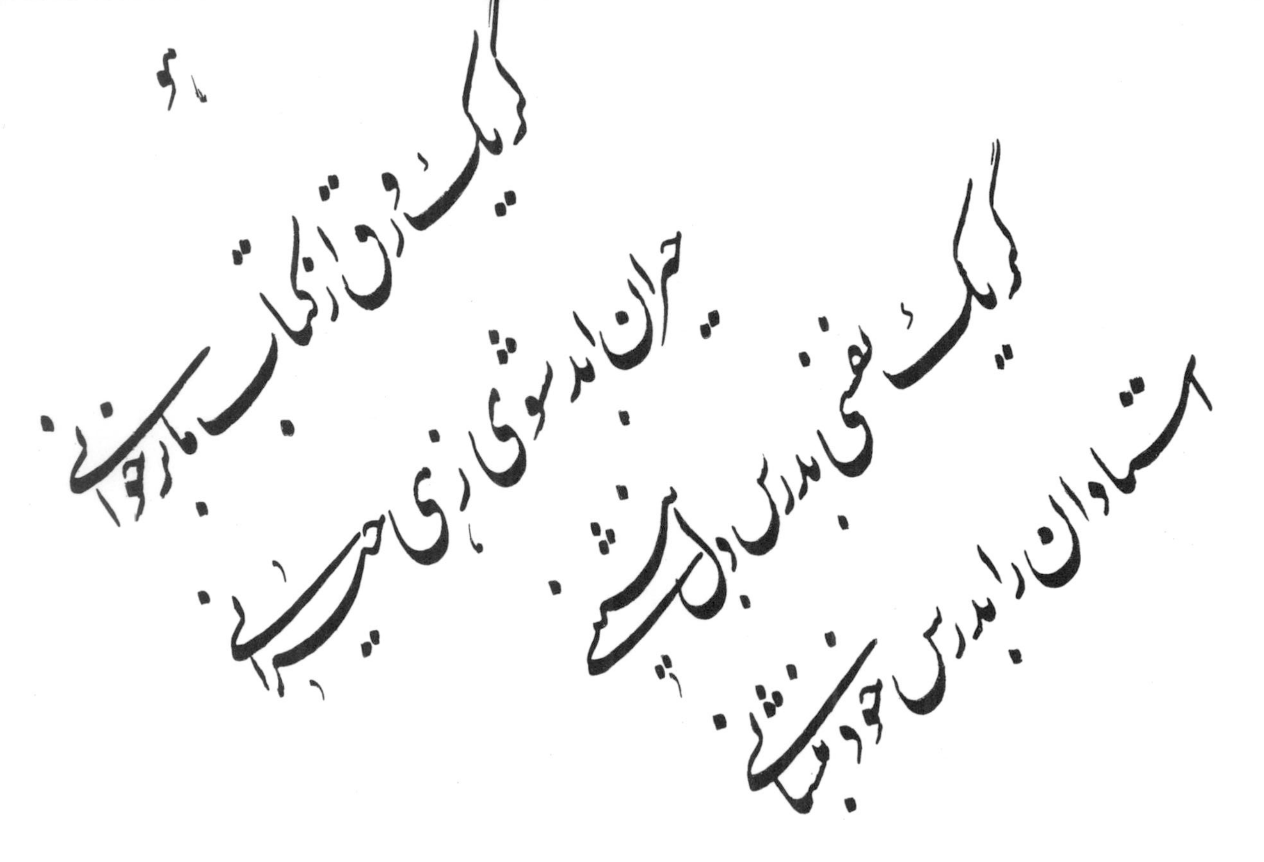
هو
گر یک ورق از کتاب ما برخوانی
حیران ابد شوی ز بی‌پایانی
گر یک نفسی بدرس دل بنشینی
استادان را بدرس خود بنشانی

One page of our book
will leave you bewildered for ever.
One real moment at the feet of the Heart
will turn your teachers into pupils.

Spirit Is Never Tired of Lovers

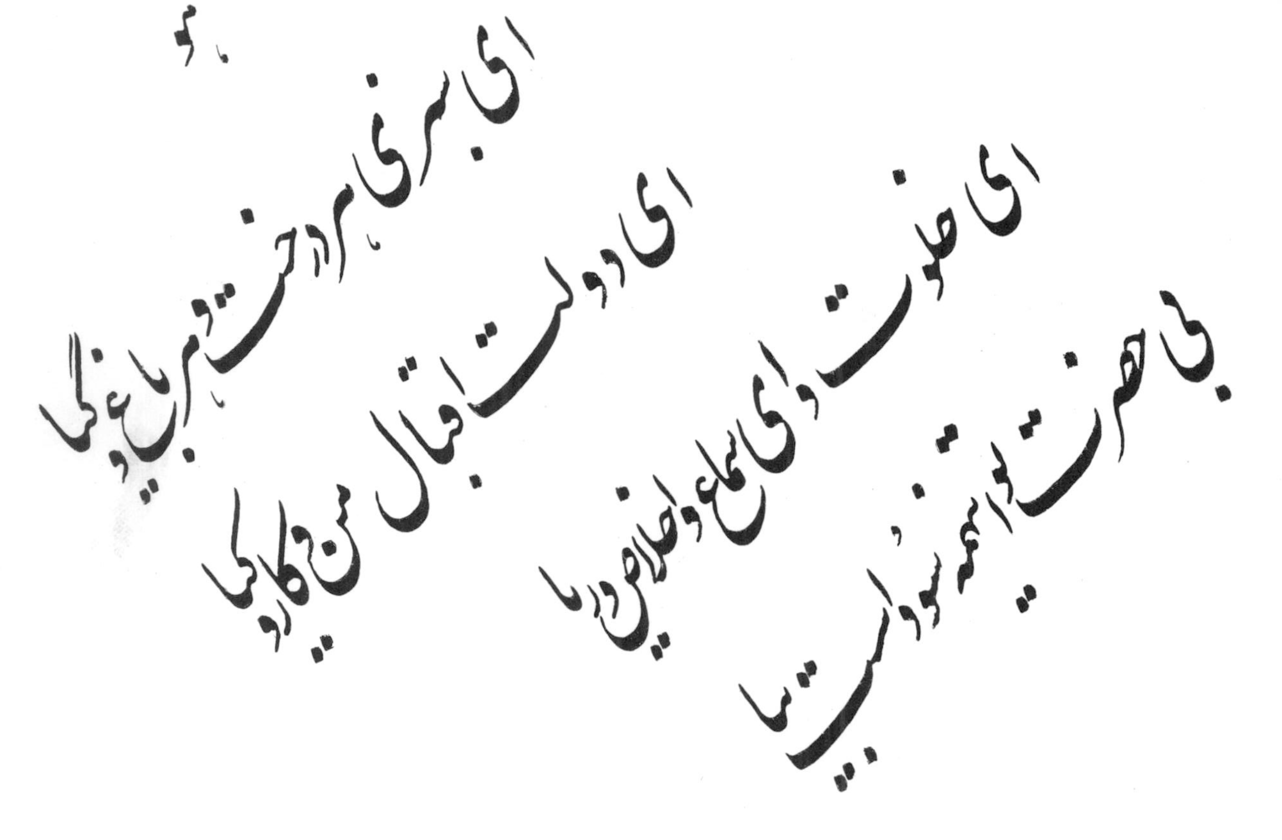
ای سبزی هر درخت و هر باغ و گیا
ای دولت اقبال من و کار و کیا
ای خلوت و ای سماع و اخلاص و ریا
بی حضرت تو همه سود است ریا

The green in every tree
is You.
The beauty of every garden
is You.
My wealth, my work, my master
is You.
Solitude, purity, pretence
is You.
There is no reality
but You.

The one You have exalted
never falls from grace.
Even the heavens bend
to kiss the feet
that You have chained.

When my soul soared
to that blessed sphere
I was free of the tyranny
of "why?" and "how?"
At last
the thousand veils lifted
and I could behold
the hidden secret.

Love came rushing
like blood in my veins
and emptied me of myself.
Now, filled with the Beloved,
I have only a name.

You are the divine word,
you mirror the majesty of the King.
All the world is contained in you.
What you are seeking is within.

O tulip, learn about colour from my face;
O Venus, learn from my heart how to play the lute.
O Destiny, when the trumpet of union sounds
come and learn about music.

A pure heart, open to the Light
will be filled with the elixir of Truth.
You may see my body
but I am only a grain of salt
dissolved in the sea of Love.

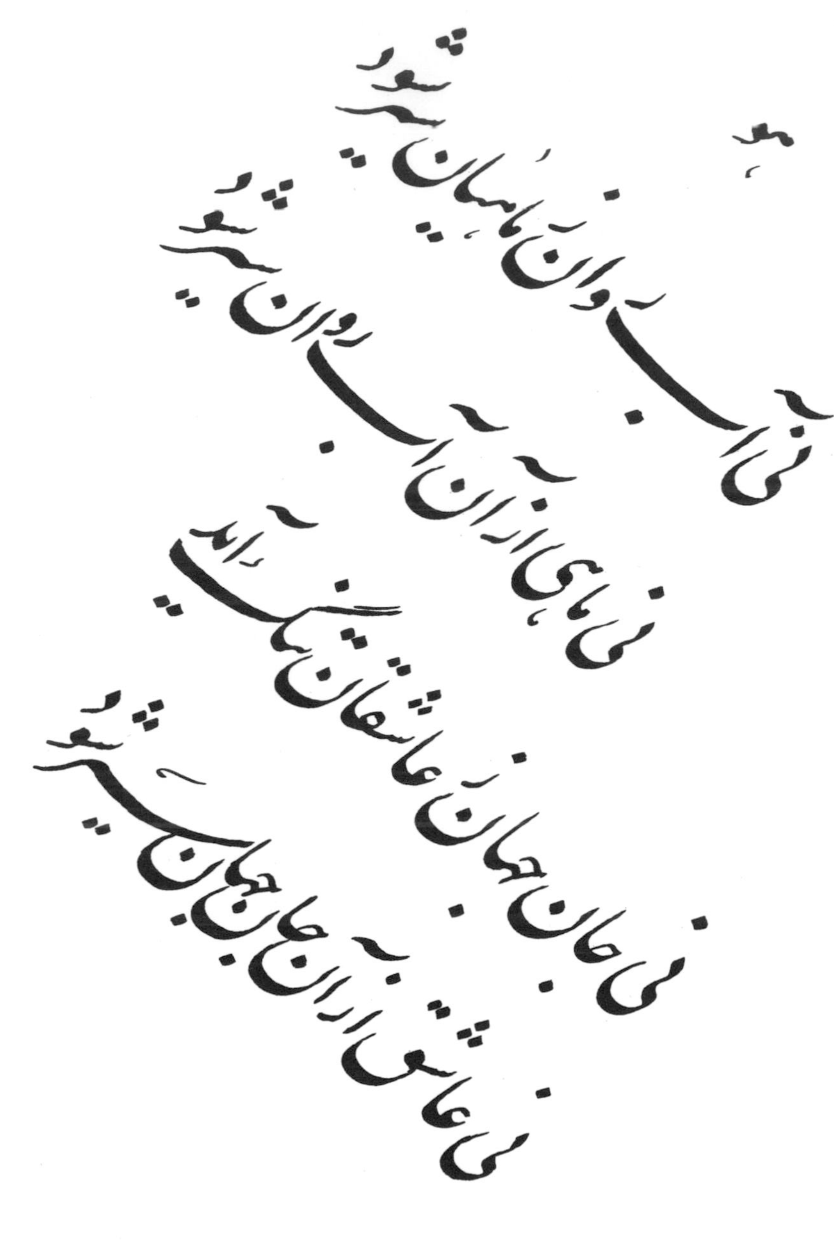

Water never tires of fish
nor do fish ever tire of water.
Spirit is never tired of lovers
nor lovers of Spirit.

We have spirit,
but what does Spirit have?
Bread feeds the hungry
but what feeds bread?
In life, anything can be exchanged
except the source of life itself.

Our horse flew on the wings of love
from the land of nothingness
and our night became illuminated
with the wine of Union.
From that wine our lips will never dry
and morning will never come.

I drank from the water of life
and all disease vanished.
I entered the garden of Union
and I found no thorns.
They say there is a doorway
from heart to heart
but what is the use of a door
when there are no walls?

Love, You are my Certainty.
You are the Creator and I, the created.
Cover the eyes of the jealous ones
when You lift me to the stars.

Today, amazed and bewildered
I have shut the door on thought
and turned to music.
There are a hundred ways
to kneel and pray
at the altar of the Beloved.

Beyond belief and disbelief
lies the vast expanse of ecstasy
where the mystic lays his head
on the cushion of Truth.

"Write me a verse," I said.

He was offended.

What can I reveal in a line or two?

"Then choose a verse for me to recite." I said.

Which verse do you think could contain me?

In the beginning
we made a special agreement
to come here
but this world of matter
is not our home.
A man may pride himself on his piety
but beyond his prayers and piety
there is another world.

When my pain became the cause of my cure
my contempt changed into reverence
and my doubt into certainty.
I see that I have been the veil on my path.
Now my body has become my heart
my heart has become my soul
and my spirit, the eternal Spirit.

There is a loneliness more precious than life.
There is a freedom more precious than the world.
Infinitely more precious than life and the world
is that moment when one is alone with God.

I found that no joy in the world
could relieve me of my sorrows, but Him.
I wanted to tell Him so many things
but when He appeared
I could not utter a word.

Seek love, seek love

for it is the gem of your essence.

Seek the One, seek the One

for He is yours for eternity.

But forbid yourself to call Him yours

for what is yours is only

the sorrow

and the longing.

In every sphere
I see the pupil of the eye,
in every pupil
I see the whole sphere.
It is the eyes of the foolish
that see one as two
while I see every two
as one.

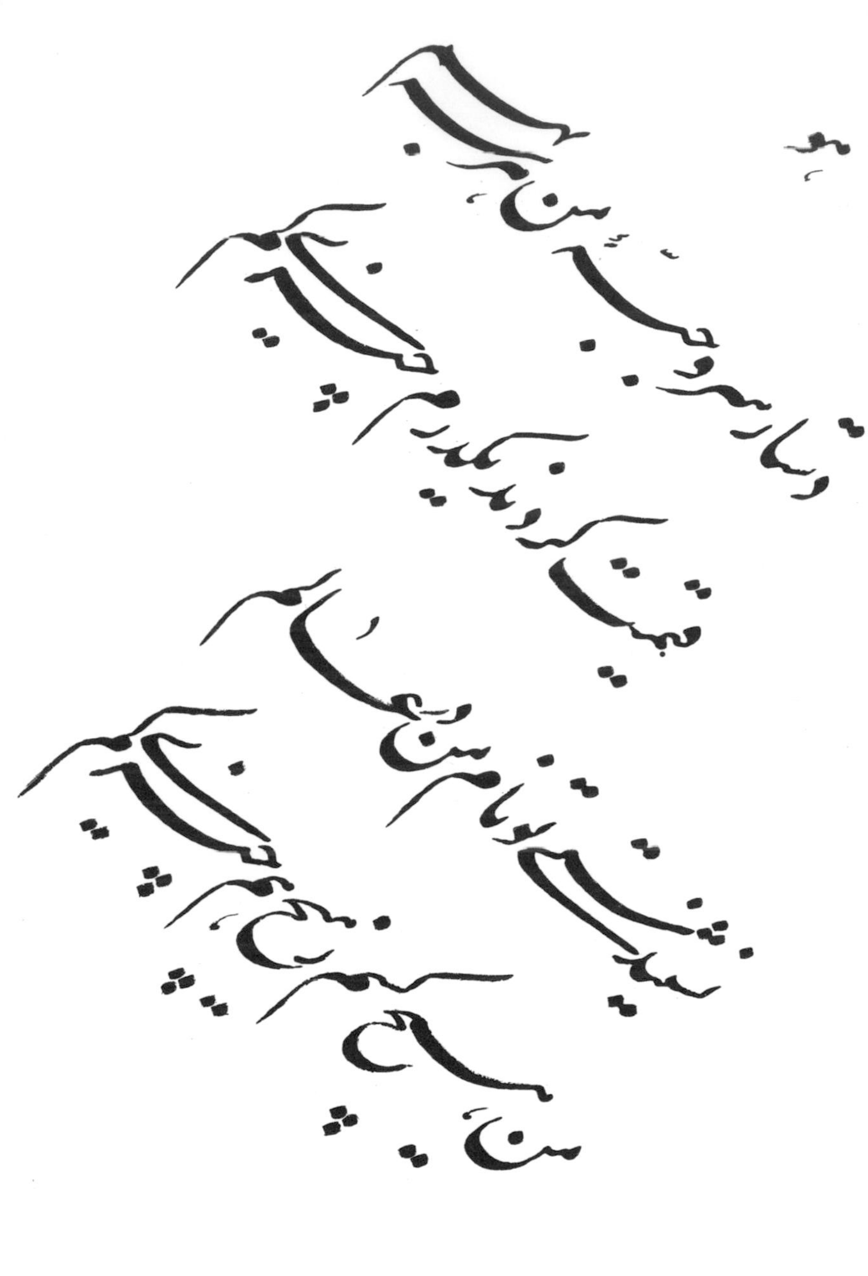

My turban, cloak and head
can be bought for less than a penny.
No one has ever heard my name.
I am nothing, nothing!

If you only knew
what bliss I find in being nothing,
you would never
advise me how to live.
When the sword of nothingness
ends my days
I will laugh at those
who mourn my death.

In Your love I grew tall;
joyous, I have risen to the skies.
They think I turn around Him
but truly I turn around Myself.

I praised you in the day

but never knew it

I slept with you at night

but never knew it

I believed I was myself

but I was You

and never knew it.

My Beloved, I do not know anymore
if I am on earth or in heaven!
Do not hand me the wine
bring it to my lips,
I am so drunk
I cannot find the way
to my mouth.

Beloved

when I look upon myself

I see that my intelligence and clarity

is You.

Everything that is precious

in my worthless being

is You.

Your Spirit dispersed the clouds
of my darkness and profanity.
Now, in the light, You sing in my heart
and dance like wine in my head.

When I walk on the path
when I enter the house of Love
I see You.
You are the King in every town.
I see You in the sun, the moon and the stars,
I see Your altar in every plant,
in every leaf.

I am bewildered by the Beloved,

He belongs to me.

Do not search elsewhere,

He lives in my heart.

I am not misleading you when I say

I am Him!

Angels dance only with You, Beloved
and only before You
do I bow in adoration.
You may accept me or not
but I will be at your feet forever.

Glorious is the man who can
distinguish the cotton of the body
from the cloth of spirit.
When Hallaj called out "I am Truth,"
it was not him who spoke,
but God!

There is another language beyond language,
another place beyond heaven and hell.
Precious gems come from another mine,
the heart draws light from another source.

In the glorious season of Union
the heart rises from the ashes
sparkling with light.
From the laughter of thunder and lightning
the clouds cry tears
that fill the garden with joy.

No one has seen
how You have risen in my chest
bright as the Moon!
No one has seen how Your Spirit
runs like blood
through my body.

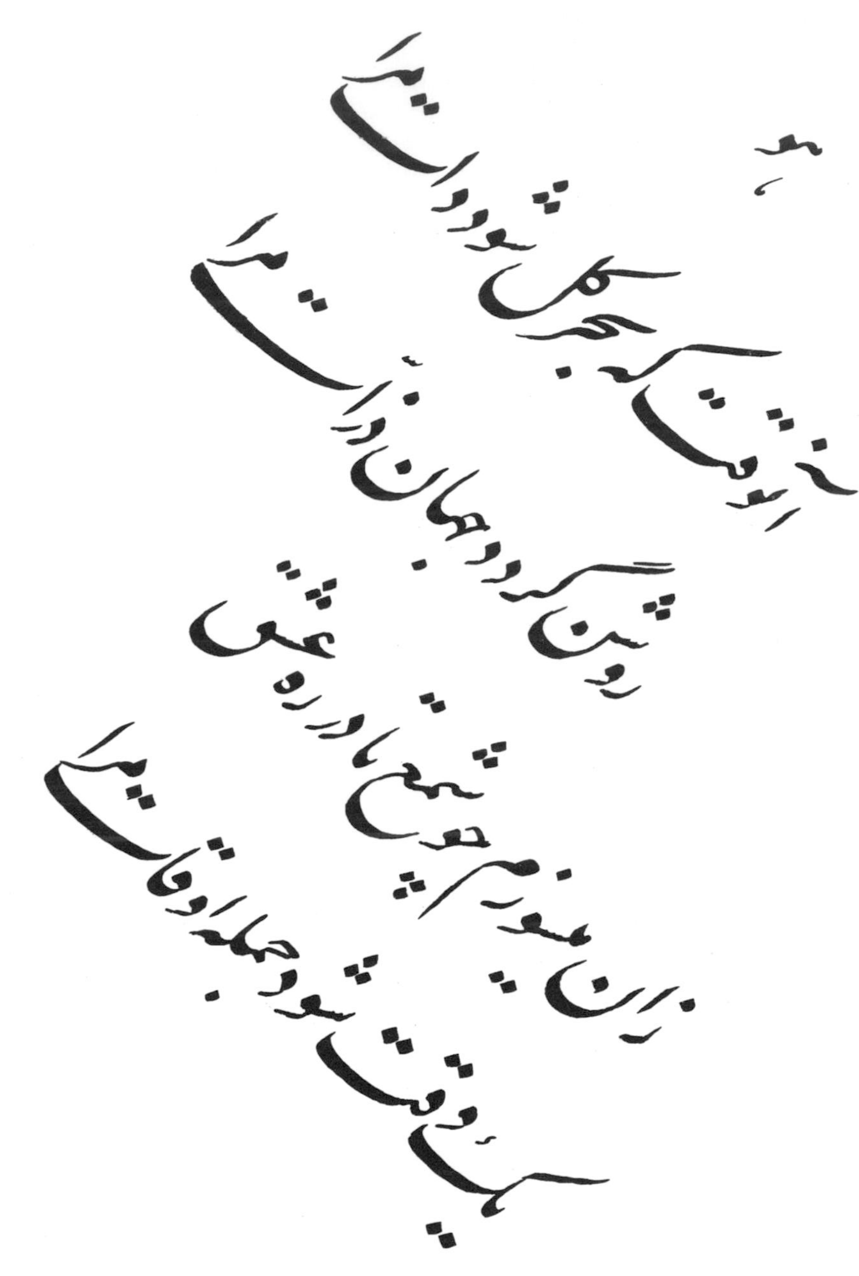

When I become the Sea
each atom flames out of me in glory.
When I am ablaze
each moment becomes Eternity.

I drank from His flaming cup
and lost my mind.
Now, like a moth, I am circling
around His Sun.

I am no longer just one drop,
I have become the entire Sea.
I speak the language of the heart
where every particle of me,
united, shouts in ecstasy!

Unless one is completely annihilated
Union is not a reality.
Union is not the merging of spirits;
the secret of Union
is the annihilation itself.

The cup I hold in my hand
is filled with the wine of Light.
It opened my eyes
and now I see the Beloved
everywhere.

The Master cut a reed from the riverbed
carved nine holes in it and called it Man.
The reed, in agony, has never stopped longing
to behold the lips that breathed into it.

What could life and the world hold
for the one who has befriended You?
In love and bewildered,
even if You offered him both worlds
what could he do with either?

On the path of Love
we are neither masters
nor the owners of our lives.
We are only a brush
in the hand
of the Master Painter.

In His spring I blossomed,
in His garden of abundance
I drank His wine
and vanished
in the splendour
of His face.

My heart saw Love
galloping alone towards the desert
and, shattered by love's majesty,
fell in love with Love.

Around the blazing Sun
the lovers whirl like specks of dust.
In the spring breeze of love
every branch that is not dry
is dancing.

The night has passed
and still we are not sober.
In the garden of the heart
the feast goes on.
The nightingale is singing
and the lover and beloved
are entwined into one.

Oh flower, what makes you smile,
the beauty of the rose garden
or the love song of the nightingale?
Or have you suddenly seen
the hidden face of the Beloved
and recognised yourself in Him?

What passed between us
in that luminous night
can never be written or told.
On my final journey
from this world
the creases of my shroud
will unfold our story.

Those beautiful words we said to one another
are hidden in the secret heart of heaven.
One day, like the rain, they will pour
our love story all over the world.

Terms & Symbolism

Beloved, Friend, King	Terms used by Rumi referring to God.
Dervish	A Sufi mystic.
Drunk, Drunkenness	Intoxication with Love.
Garden	An inner space, depicting the outward beauty of nature and the inward beauty of Spirit.
Hallaj	A Sufi, accused of heresy and executed in 922 in Baghdad for his ecstatic statements such as: Ana al Haqq, "I am Truth."
Killing	Severing the attachment to the ego.
Moon	Symbol of the heart of the mystic.
Nightingale	Symbol of the soul's longing.
Poverty	The complete annihilation of the self as a key to the attainment of Union and Truth.
Rose	Symbol of the beauty of the Beloved.
Rose-garden	Paradise and eternal Beauty.
Sufi	Mystic in search of the Beloved.

The Two Worlds	Not two separate worlds but two aspects of a continuous process. The world of matter is at one end of the spectrum while the essence, invisible to the eye, is at the other end.
Veil	Symbol of layers of the ego separating the self from the Beloved.
Whirling	Sema – Spiritual dance of the Sufis.
Wine	Symbol of the ecstatic love of God.

Index

Garden of the Soul

Garden of the Heart

Garden of the Spirit